SHARING THE
GIFT OF
ENCOURAGEMENT

CHARLES
STANLEY

OLIVER
NELSON

THOMAS NELSON PUBLISHERS
Nashville

Copyright © 1998 by Charles Stanley

All rights reserved. Written permission must be secured from the publisher to use or reproduce any part of this book, except for brief quotations in critical review or articles.

Published in Nashville, Tennessee, by Thomas Nelson, Inc.

The Bible version used in this publication is THE NEW KING JAMES VERSION. Copyright © 1979, 1980, 1982, Thomas Nelson, Inc., Publishers.

Scripture noted NASB is taken from the NEW AMERICAN STANDARD BIBLE (R), © Copyright The Lockman Foundation 1960, 1962, 1963, 1968, 1971, 1972, 1973, 1975, 1977. Used by permission.

ISBN 0-7852-7280-1

Printed in the United States of America

CONTENTS

OUR NEED FOR ENCOURAGEMENT

Every person I know could use more encouragement!

And not just a little more encouragement—a *lot* more encouragement.

For the most part, our world is experiencing a drought of encouraging words, uplifting examples, genuine heroes, "good news" stories, and genuine expressions of appreciation. Far more negative words of criticism, blame, ridicule, gossip, and backbiting hit us on a daily basis than do positive words of praise, recognition, and thankfulness.

Why is it that each of us have a deep need for encouragement, and yet so little encouragement is to be found?

I believe the foremost reason is that so few people feel encouraged in their own spirits. It is very difficult to share with others something that you do not feel yourself. Encouragement is rooted in the following:

- *self-worth*: feelings of personal value and healthy self-appreciation and self-esteem
- *dignity*: feeling as if one has a "position" in Christ
- *respect*: feeling as if one has a right to be treated as one of God's beloved children

Above all, encouragement is grounded in unconditional love. Unless a person feels truly loved for who they are and solely because they exist as a unique and valued creation of God, such a person is not, at the core of his being, going to *feel* encouraged. Such love must be received regardless of the person's actions, traits, or accomplishments. It must not be love that is granted for manipulative purposes. It must be love that is both *perceived* and actively *received* without any strings or conditions attached.

The prerequisite to encouraging others, therefore, is to feel encouraged yourself.

The Message of Encouragement

Encouragement has a very basic message: *Your past and present do not need to continue into your future.* What *is* a reality today does not need to be what *will be* the reality of tomorrow.

If you are feeling unloved . . . you can feel love.

If you are weighed down in your spirit under a load of guilt . . . you can receive forgiveness.

If you are wallowing about in a cloud of confusion . . . you can experience God's wisdom and guidance.

If your life is in turmoil . . . you can have peace in your heart.

If you are alone and rejected . . . you can be accepted and surrounded by genuine Christian friends.

If you are feeling weak and helpless . . . you can experience God's enabling presence and power.

Encouragement is speaking a word of hope. It is expressing to another person—and to yourself—the sure certainty that God created you with a greater potential for good and that God desires to help you fulfill your potential.

Your future *can* be better than your past or present.

You *can* grow and develop and be ever more transformed into the likeness of Jesus Christ.

You *can* experience greater fulfillment and wholeness than you are presently experiencing.

You *can* have an even more abundant life than the one you presently have.

Those who are discouraged tend to feel that they are locked into their present position—emotionally, spiritually, physically, materially, financially, relationally, socially, vocationally. Encouragement is saying to that imprisoned person, "God has the keys to your prison! He can make a way out of your present circumstances and situation where you do not see a way. He can help you tunnel through, climb over, or go around the obstacles in your path. He can sovereignly change hearts and remove roadblocks." Furthermore, the encourager bears the message: "Not only *can* God do these things, but I believe that He *will!*"

The message of encouragement is that we can survive the assaults of the devil against our lives, we can endure the persecution that comes our way, we can be victorious over the circumstances that assail us, and in the midst of any kind of trial, trouble, or tribulation, we can know God's peace and joy.

The message of encouragement is a triple-packed message of God's goodness, the hope we have in Christ Jesus, and the omnipotent power of the Holy Spirit at work in us, through us, and on our behalf!

The Foundation for Encouragement

On what basis is encouragement to be voiced? On the sure foundation that God loves His children and desires their highest good.

If you do not believe that God is a loving God, or if you do not believe that God is continually at work bringing all things toward an ultimate good for those who are His children through the redemptive work of Christ Jesus, then you probably are not encouraged in your own spirit—and you cannot encourage others.

On the other hand, to know that God is a loving, merciful, forgiving God—always desiring our best and working to give us His perfect good—then encouragement is within your grasp and you can share encouragement.

Before you can share encouragement with others, you must come to a firm resolve within yourself regarding what you believe about four things: (1) God's nature, (2) Jesus Christ and His work on the cross, (3) the relationship that God desires to have with His children, and (4) the work of the Holy Spirit in the world today. Encouragement flows from what you believe. It is *always* an expression of your faith in God.

Conversely, discouraging words are always an expression of a *lack of faith* in God.

Guard your words. But above all, build up your faith. The heart that is strong in faith is a heart that will naturally overflow in encouragement.

The Call to Encouragement

As Christians, we are called by God to encourage others. Time and again in the Scriptures we read that we are to "love the brotherhood" and with a fervent and pure spirit (1 Peter 1:22, 2:17). We are to build one another up in faith (Jude 20). We are to remind one another of the goodness and love of God (1 John 1:1–4).

The expression of encouragement is always to be active. We are not merely to be an encouragement to others through our example of a virtuous life. We are to *share* encouragement by voicing words of encouragement and engaging in specific deeds. Encouragement is not merely something we *are*. It is something we *do*.

Throughout the Gospels and the New Testament letters we find strong words of encouragement. Jesus is our supreme role model of encouragement. Every one of His miracle works was an act of encouragement. He described His own ministry in this way:

> The Spirit of the LORD is upon Me,
> Because He has anointed Me to preach the gospel to the poor.
> He has sent Me to heal the brokenhearted,
> To preach deliverance to the captives
> And recovery of sight to the blind,
> To set at liberty those who are oppressed,
> To preach the acceptable year of the LORD. (Luke 4:18–19)

What an encouraging world we would live in if all Christians chose to follow Christ's example and do the same: preach good news to the poor, heal the brokenhearted, proclaim freedom to the captives and recovery of sight to the blind, set free the oppressed, and proclaim the gospel of Jesus Christ, our Lord!

Jesus plainly said that He came *not* to condemn the world, but so "the world through Him might be saved" (John 3:17). The message of salvation is the most encouraging message we can ever share.

The apostle John wrote:

> I write to you, little children,
>   Because your sins are
>   forgiven you for His name's sake.
> I write to you, fathers,
>   Because you have known
>   Him who is from the beginning.
> I write to you, young men,
>   Because you have overcome
>   the wicked one.
> I write to you, little children,
>   Because you have known
>   the Father.
> I have written to you, fathers,
>   Because you have known
>   Him who is from the beginning.
> I have written to you, young men,
>   Because you are strong, and
>   the word of God abides in you,
> And you have overcome the wicked one. (1 John 2:12–14)

What wonderful words of encouragement John gave! John, who always referred to himself as the "beloved disciple," was a giver of love to others with an intent that they be built up in Christ, and in turn, love one another generously and without fear.

Again and again we see in the New Testament the message of hope, of change, of growth, of victorious living.

What we have received in Christ, and what we have been given in His Word, we are called by God to give to others. We are not called to be doomsday prophets, pessimists, down-in-the-mouth naysayers, or condemning critics. We are called to encourage!

Choose to be encouraged today.

Then choose to share encouragement.

PREPARING TO SHARE ENCOURAGEMENT

This book is for Bible study. It is not a book of happy stories or a book intended for you to use in a group setting to make others "feel good." Certainly, the gospel of Jesus Christ by itself can evoke great feelings of joy, peace, hope, contentment, and self-worth. And certainly as you share the gospel with others, you will be providing edifying encouragement. Even so, this book is not an inspirational book; it is a study manual linked to the Bible. My hope is that you will refer to your Bible again and again, and that you will freely mark phrases and words that have special meaning to you, or write in the margins what God is speaking to you in your spirit.

Many good inspirational and devotional books are on the market today. I certainly recommend that you read daily from those authors who love God's Word and help apply it to daily living in an encouraging, inspirational way. The Bible, however, will always remain the most encouraging book ever written. It is the source from which we draw our hope and faith. It is the reference to which we must return again and again to make certain that the words we speak to others are not just idle words that flow from our human desire, but rather, are words that are in line with *God's* hopes and desires.

In this study we will be focusing only on several key aspects of encouragement. As you read and study the Scriptures as a whole, you will encounter "encouragement in action" time and time again. The *whole* of God's message on encouragement cannot be contained in a Bible study book or course. It is far too great for that. It is to be found only in a full understanding of *all* of God's Word. I trust you are reading and studying the Bible on a daily basis.

Keys to Study

Repeatedly in this guide you will be asked to identify with the verses or concepts presented by answering one or more of these questions:

- What new insight have you gained?
- Have you ever had a similar experience?
- How do you feel about this?
- In what way are you challenged to act?

Insights

A spiritual insight is something that involves a new degree of understanding about the nature of God or the nature of God's relationship with you. It lies beyond a literal understanding of a fact, word, or idea. For many people, a spiritual insight comes as almost a "rush of understanding" or a "sudden seeing." It is as if a light has been turned on in a dark room. You may have read a particular passage of the Bible many times, and even studied it word by word. But then, God surprises you with a new aspect of *meaning*. That is a spiritual insight.

Insights are usually very personal. Most of them come when you see how a passage of Scripture relates to your life—perhaps something in your past, more likely something in your immediate presence, and occasionally something in your future.

Insights are a function of the Spirit of Truth—one of the names Jesus gave to the Holy Spirit. The Holy Spirit works within our spirits to reveal to us precisely what is important for us to know or understand at any given moment so that we might grow in Christ and reflect Christ to others.

Every time you study the Bible, ask the Holy Spirit to give you insights. I believe that is one prayer God delights in answering with a resounding *yes*! In fact, if you don't gain new spiritual insights after reading several passages from God's Word, you probably haven't been engaged in the process of genuine study. The person who truly studies God's Word with an open heart and an eagerness to hear from the Holy Spirit is going to have spiritual insights on a regular basis. (NOTE: There is a difference between devotional reading of the Bible—such as daily reading of a portion of Scripture—and focused Bible study, which is directed toward answering a question, understanding a concept, or identifying a recurring theme. Insights come as we engage in devotional reading of the Word, but they come more often and generally in more profound ways as we study the Bible. It is as a person *compares* one passage of Scripture with another, reading as many related passages as possible, that profound insights tend to emerge.)

As you receive spiritual insights, make notes about them. Your faith will grow when you look back in the margins of your Bible and read at a later time what God has shown you or spoken to you, and then reflect on how that insight has manifested in the subsequent months or years of your life. I recommend that you add dates to any spiritual-insight notes you make.

Experiences

We each come to God's Word with a different personal history. We come with different backgrounds in the study of the Bible and, therefore, with different levels of understanding about the Bible's content. Each person has a slightly different perspective on the Scriptures. In a group setting, these differences can sometimes cause problems.

What we all have in common are life experiences. We each can recall times in our lives when we have found the truth of a Bible passage to be highly relevant to our lives. We can cite times when the Bible confirmed, convicted, challenged, directed—and, yes, *encouraged*—us in some way. We have experiences to which we can point and say, "I know that truth in the Bible is real because of what happened to me."

Now, our experiences do not make the Bible true. The Bible is truth, period. The value of sharing our experiences is that we come to see that God's Word relates in far-reaching and amazing ways to all of human life! When we share our Bible-related experiences, we grow in our understanding that the Bible applies to *every* person, *every* aspect of human nature, and *every* human condition or problem.

Sharing experiences is important to spiritual growth. You benefit not only from hearing the experiences of others, but from sharing your own experiences. Although none of us may like the idea of sharing about times when we were discouraged or when we were a discouragement to others, these are important confessions for us to make. We have not, are not, and will not be people of encouragement at all times, in all situations, to all people. We each have a lack in this area of encouragement. There are areas in which we need to be encouraged. There are areas in which we need to grow in our ability to encourage others. Facing these facts about ourselves and confessing our shortcomings can result in our experiencing forgiveness and also in our making a new commitment to be a person of encouragement.

We also might be slightly uncomfortable sharing about times in which we have been encouraged, or times in which we have given encouragement to others. We may fear that we will come across as "bragging." Share your encouragement examples with a spirit of humility. Always point toward the reality that it is God who was the source of any encouragement you received, regardless of the instrument He may have used. Acknowledge that God was also the source of encouragement you gave to others—that you were simply an instrument in His hand. In giving God the credit for *all* encouragement, you can help build up the faith of others to trust in God to work in their lives in similar ways.

Avoid the tendency to judge others as they share their life experiences. A judgmental attitude not only can do great harm to the spiritual growth of others, but it can cause great friction within a group. Ultimately, a judgmental attitude is a major roadblock both

to your receiving encouragement in your own life and your giving of encouragement to others. We rarely speak encouraging words
to those we are judging in our hearts!

Listen. Discuss. Talk about what the Scriptures say and mean to
you. Be careful to do so in a way that is *encouraging.*

Emotional Response

Just as we each have unique personal histories, so do we have
our own emotional responses to the Bible. No emotional response
is more valid than another. One person may be very convicted by
a particular passage. Another may feel great relief at reading the
same words! Face your emotions honestly and give others the freedom to share their emotions fully. Every emotion is valid.

Again, our emotions do not give validity to the Scriptures. Neither should they be used as a gauge of faith. Our faith must always
be based on what God says, not on what we feel. The Scriptures
are true regardless of the emotions they evoke in us. The value of
sharing emotional responses is this: We grow in our understanding that every time we approach the Scriptures, we must invite God
to work in our emotions as we read. If we approach the Scriptures
in a totally emotionless, coldly intellectual way, we are not going
to *feel encouraged* by what we read. Encouragement is a feeling. It
is a response God desires for you to have as you read portions of
His Word.

Bible study groups sometimes become sidetracked as individu-
als within them share opinions. Opinions tend to divide people.
They lead to debate, distrust, and confusion. Keep your group
focused on the sharing of feelings and experiences, not opinions.
Do not allow your group sessions to degenerate into a debate about
God's Word.

Also make certain that your sharing does not take on an air of
admonition. Leave it to God to challenge a person to become an
encourager and to give up discouraging ways.

Certainly scholarly commentaries have a place in the study and
teaching of the Bible. But a person's knowledge and opinion actually have little impact on other people within the context of a group
Bible study. What God says to us individually and directly is what
we each find to be truly significant. And God often speaks to us in

the language of the heart—the silent language of intuition, inner-most desires, unvoiced longings, and deep emotions. When we share feelings with one another, we grow closer together. When we share only opinions, we rarely grow closer as a community or find unity of spirit in Christ Jesus.

Challenges

As we read the Bible, we ultimately come to those passages, or receive insights, that challenge us to change something in our lives.

The challenge may be a conviction to give up something, such as a sin we may have been harboring. We may feel a need to correct something in the way we think or the way we act toward others. We may feel a deep, compelling desire to make things right with another person. Especially as you study the topic of encouragement, you may feel a conviction that you have been a source of discouragement to another person. You may be challenged in your spirit to go to that person to apologize for "pulling them down" in their emotions.

The challenge of God may also be a clear call to do something new—to acquire a new habit or to begin a new form of ministry to others. In my life God never ceases to challenge me just beyond my ability so that I must always rely on Him to work in me and through me. God is never content with the status quo; He always wants us to grow more like His Son, Jesus Christ. As I read the Scriptures and hear others share their life experiences and emotional responses to the Word, I often feel challenged to grow as they have grown or to extend myself to others as they have extended themselves. I believe it is vitally important for us to be aware of the ways God may speak to us through the Bible to challenge us, stretch us, change us, or cause our faith to grow.

In your study of encouragement, you may very well feel a direct challenge from God to go to a specific person and give a word of encouragement or to do something of an encouraging nature for another person. Be open and receptive to that call. Do not sweep it under the rug of your conscience or file it away. Act on that challenge. God is calling you to be an encourager, and as you obey His challenge, He will not only teach you more about encouragement, but He will cause a spirit of encouragement to flood your own heart and mind!

God's ultimate reason for us to know His Word is that we might share His Word with others, in both actions and words. God not only expects us to know and believe the Bible, He expects us to *do* His Word—to keep His commandments, to be His witnesses, and to carry on His mission in the world (James 1:22).

God expects us to learn about encouragement so that we can be encouraged and be encouragers. Look for Him to challenge you repeatedly as you read His Word and study these lessons.

Personal or Group Study?

This book is designed for group study. If you don't have an existing group of people with whom you can talk about your insights, experiences, emotions, and challenges, I encourage you to explore ways in which you might create a Bible study group. You may be able to start a Bible study in your home, using this book as a focal point. Perhaps you can talk to your pastor about organizing a Bible study group in your church. There is much to be learned on your own. There is much *more* to be learned as you become part of a small group that desires to grow in the Lord.

If you are not able to generate a group for this study, I encourage you to find at least one other person with whom you can either share this study or share the fruit of what you learn and experience as a result of personal study. This may be a spouse, a child, or a close friend. It may be a person at your church with whom you have a special bond of fellowship or prayer.

You'll find personal benefit in giving voice to what you have learned. Focus on how the Word of God is encouraging you and on ways in which you are feeling challenged to encourage others.

Keep the Bible Central

The tendency of a group studying encouragement is to try to be a group in which all statements are happy and upbeat. A group of people can become so concerned about being encouragers that they squelch any serious, thoughtful, or confessional statements, as well as stifle any statements of honest doubt. The result is that the group remains only at the "surface level" of expressing feelings, insights, challenges, and experiences.

The Bible calls a person—and a group—to explore its depths. The deep riches of God's Truth are not to be found at the surface level. Voice your questions, concerns, and challenges to one another. And then listen for answers from God's Word.

Keep the Bible at the center of all you do. Do not allow your group to become an arena for personal counseling or a forum for sharing jokes and lighthearted anecdotes. Stay focused on God's Word.

Prayer

As you begin your Bible study, ask God to give you spiritual ears to hear what He wants you to hear and to give you spiritual eyes to see what He wants you to see. Ask Him to give you new insights, to bring to your memory the experiences that relate to what you read, and to help you identify clearly your emotional responses to His Word. Ask Him to reveal to you what He desires for you to be, say, and do.

At the close of your study time, ask the Lord to seal to your heart and mind the material you have studied so that you will never forget it and you will always desire to apply it. Ask Him to transform you more into the likeness of Jesus Christ as you meditate later on what you have studied. Above all, ask Him to give you the courage to become, say, and do what He challenges you to become, say, and do!

As you pray, open yourself up to new ways in which you might be encouraged and be an encourager. Be keenly aware that God desires this for you. He will speak to you not only as you study His Word, but as you pray about what you have studied.

Now, consider these questions:

- *What new insights into encouragement do you hope to gain from this study? (Are there questions about encouragement that you desire to have answered, are there desires of your heart that you hope to have met?)*

_____

_____

• *In what ways have you struggled or succeeded with encouragement in the past? (Have you been the recipient of discouragement? Of encouragement? Do you recognize that you have been a source of discouragement to others? Have you been a source of encouragement?)*

_____

_____

• *How do you feel today about God's call on your life to be encouraged and to be an encourager? Do you have any fears about sharing encouragement with others?*

_____

_____

• *Are you genuinely open to being challenged in this area? Do you have a desire to be of greater encouragement to others?*

_____

_____

LESSON 2

YOU ARE GOD'S BELOVED

God loves you. Let the words sink into your spirit. They are three of the most encouraging words you can ever hear or speak.

People in our world today are starving for people to tell them that God loves them. Most people receive very little affirmation in their lives and very little love. Adults have readily confessed to me with tears in their eyes, "I never heard my father say he loves me," or, "I know my mother must have loved me because of what she did for me, but after about age ten, I don't recall my mother ever telling me she loved me."

I know how they feel. My father died when I was only nine months old, and so I have no recollection of his telling me he loved me. My mother married my stepfather—a hard and critical man—when I was nine years old, and I never heard him say he loved me. Neither did I ever receive anything from him that was presented with affection or personal concern. I know the loneliness in spirit that can develop if a person grows up aching to hear unspoken words of approval, affection, and love.

For years in my ministry, I did not "feel" the love of God in my heart. I knew He loved me on the basis of His Word, but I did not have a "feeling" that He loved me. It was long after I was adult and had been a pastor for many years that I had an experience in which I truly felt the love of God filling my heart. It was an experience I wish every person could have. There's nothing as glorious this side of heaven as knowing that God loves you with an infinite, unconditional love and that it is out of His love that He has created you, forgiven you, and receives you fully as His beloved child.

The Hallmarks of God's Love

Let me share with you two great truths about God's love for you:

1. *God loves each one of us unconditionally and absolutely.* God's love is absolute, and it does not change over time or according to *your* behavior. God's love is not influenced by circumstances or situations, and it cannot be diminished. God can never love you more than He loves you today, and neither can He love you less. He loves you solely on the basis that He created you, and He chooses to love you—now and every moment of your life.

Nothing that you do, or that happens to you, can separate you from God's love (Rom. 8:35–39).

2. *God loves us first.* God does not wait for us to come to Him with an expression of love before He extends love to us. To the contrary! God loves us first. John said it simply and eloquently: "We love Him because He first loved us" (1 John 4:19).

God is always waiting with open arms, ready to receive those who turn to Him. He longs to embrace us, forgive us, restore us to full fellowship with Him, and to bless us as His children.

What the Word Says	What the Word Says to Me
Who shall separate us from the love of Christ? Shall tribulation, or distress, or persecution, or famine, or nakedness, or peril, or sword? . . . Yet in all these things we are more than conquerors through Him who loved us. For I am persuaded that neither death nor life, nor angels nor principalities nor powers, nor things present nor	_____ _____ _____ _____ _____ _____ _____ _____ _____

things to come, nor height nor
depth, nor any other created
thing, shall be able to separate us
from the love of God which is in
Christ Jesus our Lord. (Rom.
8:35, 37–39)

What an encouraging word, that nothing—absolutely nothing—can separate us from God's love for us. His love is always extended to you and to me. It is our responsibility to accept His love, receive it, and delight in it. Those who do so enjoy an inner freedom and level of self-worth that they cannot experience by any other means.

- *Have you had an experience in which you received God's love and forgiveness?*

- *How do you feel in knowing that God loves you unconditionally, absolutely, and "first"?*

Why Some Don't Believe God Loves Them

There are no doubt a number of reasons that people fail to feel or experience the love of God, but in this lesson, I want to focus on three of them. Often when we seek to encourage another person who is "down" in spirit, we will find one of these factors at the root of their discouragement. People do not believe God loves them because:

- They have never had a role model of God's love.
- They have been taught incorrectly about God.

• They have gone through difficulties that they believe a loving God could, would, or should have spared them from experiencing.

Lack of Role Models

My lack of understanding about God's love came largely from a lack of role models. I knew my mother loved me, but she was the only person in my childhood that I knew with certainty loved me to the point of *being there for me* if times were tough—which they frequently were for us.

It isn't enough to have someone tell you that he or she loves you. The person must *be there for you* when you need him or her. We each need to experience love in tangible, physical forms. We need the presence, comfort, and touch of other people.

We especially need this when we are experiencing pain, suffering, depression, rejection, loneliness, tragedies, crises, sickness, and hard times. We need love that has "arms" that will hug us, hold us, comfort us, and say, "God loves you, and so do I."

• *Can you recall a time in your life when you were discouraged and someone expressed love to you not only in words, but in their physical presence? How did you feel?*

_____

_____

Jesus knew this human need for an abiding presence of love. He spent much of His last evening before the crucifixion *commanding* His disciples to "love one another" (John 15:17).

One of the central teachings in the early church was that Christians were to be role models of God's love one to another. John wrote, "If God so loved us, we also ought to love one another" (1 John 4:11).

If you have never experienced the love of God through other people, then find a fellowship of Christian believers where that love is flowing freely, purely, and in actuality, not just in lip service. Find a church where people are serving one another and ministering to one another with a loving attitude.

Choose also to be an agent of God's love. Be a role model for others of God's loving presence.

• *Have you had a good role model for God's love in your life?*

_____

_____

What the Word Says	What the Word Says to Me
[Jesus said]: "These things I have spoken to you, that My joy may remain in you, and that your joy may be full. This is My commandment, that you love one another as I have loved you. Greater love has no one than this, than to lay down one's life for his friends." (John 15:11–13)	_____ _____ _____ _____ _____ _____ _____ _____
Beloved, let us love one another, for love is of God; and everyone who loves is born of God and knows God. (1 John 4:7)	_____ _____ _____ _____

Incorrect Teaching

Many people have grown up from their childhoods with a false understanding of God. If you are such a person, I invite you today to *relearn* what you believe to be true about God. God is *not* a harsh judge with a long, white beard, sitting on His throne just waiting to pounce on you for doing wrong. That is a picture that has been painted by some people, but that is not the picture that is presented in the New Testament! The Bible teaches us that God's very nature—His essence, His personality—is love. God's mercy always balances God's righteousness (1 John 4:14–16).

The psalmist speaks repeatedly of God's loving kindness. It is on the basis of God's love that we can hope for God's salvation, ongoing provision, and deliverance in times of trouble (Ps. 36:7–8, 10–11).

The motivation for God's sending Jesus into the world was love. The most famous verse in all the Bible assures us of this: "God so loved the world that He gave His only begotten Son" (John 3:16).

God desires to reveal Himself to you today as a loving Father—one who will protect you, provide for you, forgive you, help you, bless you, encourage you, and uplift you. His arms are open wide to you. He longs to shower His love and good gifts upon you and for you to live with Him forever. He also longs to be loved *by* you. He wants to be in a loving relationship with you so that you share your heart fully with Him and He, in turn, shares Himself fully with you.

What encouraging news to our soul, and what encouraging news to share with others!

- *In your life, have you received correct teaching about the loving nature of God?*

_____

_____

What the Word Says

God is love, and he who abides in love abides in God, and God in him. (1 John 4:16b)

How precious is Your lovingkindness, O God!
Therefore the children of men put their trust under the shadow of Your wings.
They are abundantly satisfied with the fullness of Your house,
And You give them drink from the river of Your pleasures. . . . Oh, continue Your lovingkindness to those who know You,

What the Word Says to Me

_____

_____

_____

_____

_____

_____

_____

_____

_____

_____

_____

_____

_____

And Your righteousness to the
upright in heart.
Let not the foot of pride come
against me,
And let not the hand of the
wicked drive me away.
(Ps. 36:7–8, 10–11)

All Things for Good

A third reason that people do not believe God loves them is because they have a false understanding of how God might use difficulties that come into a person's life. They falsely believe God to be the source, or instigator, of trouble. They end up blaming God for every tragedy, disappointment, or crisis that comes their way. They ask, "How could God love me and allow this terrible thing to happen to me?"

The Bible teaches very clearly that good and bad times happen to believers and unbelievers alike. No person is immune from life's circumstances, both positive and negative (Matt. 5:45). We live in a fallen world in which both evil and good exist. At no time are we told that God spares Christians from all temptations, trials, or problems. What we can be assured is that God is *with* us and remains with us when trouble strikes and that God can use the trial or difficulty to accomplish a good purpose in our lives. In several places in the Scriptures, God assures His people that He will never leave them nor forsake them (Deut. 31:6, 8; Josh. 1:5; Heb. 13:5).

God desires for us to be whole—spirit, mind, and body—and His purposes for us are always for our ultimate good (3 John 2 and Rom. 8:28 below). When we experience a time of difficulty, our first question should not be "Why me, God?" but rather, "God, what good are you desiring to work in me and through me?" God's purpose in allowing difficulty into our lives is so that He might either correct us from error or further refine in us those things that are good. We are constantly in a state of being:

- *purified*—all impurities of sin being burned away from us—or
- *perfected*—all good things in us being strengthened.

The process of purification or correction is called "chastisement" or "chastening" in the Scriptures. When we are being chastened, God is calling us to turn away from things that are evil or harmful. He does not want us to suffer the terrible consequences of sin.

We are assured that "whom the LORD loves He chastens" (Heb. 12:6). God's process is not one of *punishment*, which is a response to negative behavior, but of *correction*, which has a teaching component to it. God's intent is that we learn a positive lesson so that we might change our ways, grow spiritually, and put ourselves into a position to receive an even greater blessing from our loving heavenly Father. Just as any loving parent, God corrects us and teaches us *for our good.*

The perfecting process is one of ongoing learning; in times of difficulty, the LORD brings to strength those character traits in us that are godly. It is in times of trouble that we learn in a focused way how to apply God's wisdom, love, and power. In many ways, the traits of self-control, endurance in faith, and true godliness are forged in the fires of suffering (2 Peter 1:5–8). The purpose of God in perfecting us is that we might become more useful servants in God's kingdom—our witness might be brighter, our service more productive and effective. God loves us enough to want us to grow up into the very likeness of Jesus Christ, His beloved Son!

What the Word Says	What the Word Says to Me
He makes His sun to rise on the evil and on the good, and sends rain on the just and on the unjust. (Matt. 5:45)	_____ _____ _____ _____
I will not leave you nor forsake you. (Josh. 1:5)	_____ _____
And we know that all things work together for good to those who love God, to those who are the called according to His purpose. (Rom. 8:28)	_____ _____ _____ _____ _____

Beloved, I pray that you may
prosper in all things and be in
health, just as your soul prospers.
(3 John 2)

And you have forgotten the exhor-
tation which speaks to you as to
sons:
"My son, do not despise the chastening of the LORD,
Nor be discouraged when you are
rebuked by Him;
For whom the LORD loves He
chastens,
And scourges every son whom He
receives." (Heb. 12:5–6)

But also for this very reason, giving all diligence, add to your faith
virtue, to virtue knowledge, to
knowledge self-control, to self-
control perseverance, to
perseverance godliness, to godliness brotherly kindness, and to
brotherly kindness love. For if
these things are yours and
abound, you will be neither barren
nor unfruitful in the knowledge of
our Lord Jesus Christ. (2 Peter
1:5–8)

• *What new insights do you have into God's nature of love?*

• *In what ways are you feeling challenged to share a message of
God's love with another person? What is the most loving way in
which you might share that message?*

YOU CAN RECEIVE FORGIVENESS

Y ou can be forgiven! No matter what sin you have committed, you can be cleansed of that sin by God. No matter how much guilt and shame you feel, you can be forgiven and have a newness of spirit. God's Word is absolute on these truths.

The assurance of God's ever-present and free offer of forgiveness is one of the most encouraging truths of God that a person can ever share. It is through forgiveness that we genuinely experience a newness of life and are given the gift of eternal life.

The Nature of God's Forgiveness

There are five great truths about God's forgiveness that I want to focus on in this lesson:

1. God's forgiveness is offered to all, but it must be actively received.
2. God's provision for forgiveness is the shed blood of Jesus Christ.
3. When we receive God's forgiveness, we are given a new spiritual nature.
4. When God forgives, God forgets.
5. In our relationships with others, we experience forgiveness *as* we forgive those who have wronged us.

Receiving God's Gift of Forgiveness

God's forgiveness is extended to all, but not everybody receives God's forgiveness. God's forgiveness is offered freely, but it is not experienced in a person's life without a conscious, deliberate act of acceptance.

There are those who seem to believe that God automatically and universally forgives everybody. That is not the message of the Bible. God's forgiveness must be *received*. This is an act of the human will. Part of God's creation of us is that we have the privilege to refuse or to accept God's offer of forgiveness and love—we are not forced to receive forgiveness. Neither are we automatically forgiven. We must turn to God and actively and intentionally receive forgiveness.

To receive God's forgiveness, one must first acknowledge within oneself the need for forgiveness and reconciliation to God. When we confess to ourselves and to God that we are in need of forgiveness and turn to Him to receive forgiveness, He grants forgiveness freely and unconditionally (1 John 1:9).

What the Word Says	What the Word Says to Me
If we confess our sins, He is faithful and just to forgive us our sins and to cleanse us from all unrighteousness. (1 John 1:9)	_____ _____ _____ _____
He who believes in Him [Jesus] is not condemned; but he who does not believe is condemned already, because he has not believed in the name of the only begotten Son of God. And this is the condemnation, that the light has come into the world, and men loved darkness rather than light, because their deeds were evil. (John 3:18–19)	_____ _____ _____ _____ _____ _____ _____ _____ _____ _____

Jesus' Death Makes Forgiveness Possible

God's offer of forgiveness is based upon the sacrificial death of Jesus Christ. When Adam and Eve sinned against God through their willful disobedience in the Garden of Eden, they caused all of mankind to be plunged into sin. Every person is born with a sin nature that separates the person spiritually from God.

God provided a bridge over this sin-nature chasm: In the Old Testament, this bridge was in the form of animal sacrifices. The shedding of blood—the foremost symbol of life—was required for the forgiveness of sin. God required man to recognize in a very tangible form that He is the author of all life and that no true wholeness of life can be experienced apart from Him.

The supreme and definitive sacrifice for sin was made when God offered His own Son, Jesus Christ, on the cross. When Jesus died on the cross, shedding His blood as a sin-free "lamb" without any blemish, He took unto Himself the sins of the world. His sacrificial death eliminated any further need for the blood sacrifice of animals. The blood of Jesus purchased salvation from sin once and for all time. Jesus said of Himself and His death on the cross:

> As Moses lifted up the serpent in the wilderness, even so must the Son of Man be lifted up, that whoever believes in Him should not perish but have eternal life. (John 3:14–15)

In the Old Testament, a plague of deadly vipers came upon the children of Israel as they wandered in the wilderness between Egypt and the Land of Promise, and God commanded Moses to make a bronze serpent and place it on a pole. All who were bitten by a viper and then looked upon the bronze serpent with faith in God survived the plague. Those who did not look with faith in God to overcome evil on their behalf died (Num. 21:1–9). Jesus said that in like manner, He would be lifted up on the cross so that all who "looked" on Him with faith would be saved from their sin nature and receive the gift of eternal spiritual life (John 3:16).

Jesus Christ is God's *means* for receiving His forgiveness. He has made no other provision. Jesus said very plainly that He was the "way" to salvation (John 14:6).

What the Word Says	What the Word Says to Me
For God so loved the world that He gave His only begotten son, that whoever believes in Him should not perish but have everlasting life. For God did not send His Son into the world to condemn the world, but that the world through Him might be saved. (John 3:16–17)	_____ _____ _____ _____ _____ _____ _____ _____ _____
[Jesus said]: "I am the way, the truth, and the life. No one comes to the Father except through Me." (John 14:6)	_____ _____ _____ _____
[Jesus said]: I am the door. If anyone enters by Me, he will be saved, and will go in and out and find pasture. (John 10:9)	_____ _____ _____ _____

• *What new insights do you have into God's provision for forgiveness?*

_____

_____

God Forgives the Old and Gives the New

When we receive God's forgiveness, we are given a completely new nature. God forgives the old, and then gives the new! Our old spiritual nature—with all of its desire for self and sin—is cleansed from us. Our hearts are made new, and our new spiritual nature has a desire for God and a desire to follow His commandments. This change in our spiritual nature is so complete that the best way one can describe it is that we are "born again" in our spirits—we are birthed anew, we are begotten again (John 3:5–8).

When a baby is born, it has no memory of what it was like to be a fetus. Everything about the baby's life is changed at birth: the

baby breathes air, experiences the weight of gravity, and has a completely new sensation of touch. It cries, takes in nourishment through its mouth, grows in self-awareness and awareness of others, sees light, and experiences many other changes. The same is true for the person who is born anew spiritually. Everything about one's spiritual perception and experience is changed!

What the Word Says	What the Word Says to Me
Jesus answered, "Most assuredly, I say to you, unless one is born of water and the Spirit, he cannot enter the kingdom of God. That which is born of the flesh is flesh, and that which is born of the Spirit is spirit. Do not marvel that I said to you, 'You must be born again.' The wind blows where it wishes, and you hear the sound of it, but cannot tell where it comes from and where it goes. So is everyone who is born of the Spirit." (John 3:5–8)	
Blessed be the God and Father of our Lord Jesus Christ, who according to His abundant mercy has begotten us again. (1 Peter 1:3)	
Therefore, if anyone is in Christ, he is a new creation; old things have passed away; behold, all things have become new. (2 Cor. 5:17)	
Though your sins are like scarlet, They shall be as white as snow; Though they are red like crimson They shall be as wool. (Is. 1:18)	

God Forgives and Forgets

When God forgives, God forgets. Forgiveness from God results in a complete "fresh start" from God's perspective. Nothing of the old is remembered or counted against a person.

No matter how many times a person errs or sins against God after he or she is saved, a person can be forgiven and experience a new beginning. Any time we turn to God with a sincere heart and admit our failures, shortcomings, and willful rebellion, God hears our prayer and responds with forgiveness. Once we are forgiven, we stand before God totally cleansed. God never holds our past sin against us.

What the Word Says	What the Word Says to Me
You have lovingly delivered my soul from the pit of corruption, For You have cast all my sins behind Your back. (Is. 38:17)	----------------------------- ----------------------------- ----------------------------- -----------------------------
As far as the east is from the west, So far has He removed our transgression from us. (Ps. 103:12)	----------------------------- ----------------------------- -----------------------------

Forgiven As We Forgive

Some people live with guilt, shame, remorse, and other lingering negative feelings of anger and bitterness *not* because they have failed to believe in Jesus Christ or failed to receive God's forgiveness but because they have not forgiven other people who have wronged them, hurt them, or rejected them. God's Word is very clear on this: "Forgive, and you will be forgiven" (Luke 6:37). When we forgive others, releasing them from our hearts, we experience great freedom of spirit.

Heaviness of heart is not necessarily a product of sin against God. It can be the result of holding a grudge, continuing to bear resentment, or harboring bitterness against others. Hate and a spirit of vengeance can weigh down the soul. Choose to be free! Forgive those who have done evil against you. Entrust them to God.

What the Word Says	What the Word Says to Me
[Jesus said]: "Judge not, and you shall not be judged. Condemn not, and you shall not be condemned. Forgive, and you will be forgiven." (Luke 6:37)	------------------------------ ------------------------------ ------------------------------ ------------------------------ ------------------------------
[Jesus said]: "And whenever you stand praying, if you have anything against anyone, forgive him, that your Father in heaven may also forgive you your trespasses. But if you do not forgive, neither will your Father in heaven forgive your trespasses." (Mark 11:25–26)	------------------------------ ------------------------------ ------------------------------ ------------------------------ ------------------------------ ------------------------------ ------------------------------ ------------------------------ ------------------------------

- *Have you ever experienced the freedom of forgiveness after forgiving another person?*

_____

_____

- *How do you feel about God's command that we forgive others in order to be forgiven?*

_____

_____

What encouraging news that God makes a way for every person to experience freedom from guilt and shame. God freely offers forgiveness to all who face up to their sin, believe in the sacrificial death of Jesus Christ, and accept what Jesus did as having been on their behalf.

What encouraging news to know that God has made a provision for each of us to have a completely new spiritual nature!

What encouraging news that God does not hold our sins against us once we have received forgiveness! He forgets our past and makes a provision for *all* things to be new for us.

If you encounter people who are suffering under guilt, are mired in sin, or can't seem to let go of their past, give them the good news: "God wants to forgive you and give you a new life in Christ Jesus!"

- *Have you experienced God's offer of forgiveness? How did you feel when you received God's forgiveness of your sin nature?*

   _____

   _____

- *What new insights do you have into forgiveness?*

   _____

   _____

- *In what ways are you being challenged to share this encouraging news of God's forgiveness with another person? Is God bringing to your mind a specific person who might need this word of encouragement today?*

   _____

   _____

Three Lies That Keep People from Forgiveness

Satan is the father of all lies, and some of his foremost lies relate to God's forgiveness. Above all else, Satan does not want a person to receive God's forgiveness or to be given the gifts of a new nature and eternal life. Three of his lies are these:

1. You are a good person, and therefore you do not need to be forgiven.
2. Your sins are too great, too horrible, to be forgiven.
3. Your sins have been repeated too often to be forgiven.

Every Person Needs Forgiveness

Satan's first lie against a person is usually an attempt to convince the person that he doesn't *need* salvation. He whispers to the heart,

"You're OK. You haven't done anything wrong. Everybody makes mistakes. In fact, in comparison to other people, you haven't done anything all that bad."

God's Word says that every person is in need of forgiveness. We all are born with a sin nature that is in need of being changed (Rom. 3:23). We all err in keeping God's commandments—sometimes out of ignorance, and sometimes willfully and rebelliously. To claim that we don't have a sin nature or that we do not sin is sheer folly. (1 John 1:6, 8).

God does not grade "on the curve" or on the average. He judges the nature of mankind as being either forgiven or unforgiven. You cannot be good enough, or do enough good deeds, to earn God's forgiveness. God's forgiveness is always a gift, never something we can achieve by our own efforts (Eph. 2:8–9).

Sometimes a person will suffer with guilt and shame, and yet attempt to justify their position in saying, "But I don't deserve this guilt and shame. I'm a *good person.*" The most loving and encouraging thing you can say to such a person is this: "We are all sinners. Sin results in our feeling guilt, shame, and a sense of being 'unclean.' But thank God, He has made a way for each of us to be free from the weight of sin!"

For many people, the news that they don't need to earn their own salvation—that they don't need to strive, to work, to struggle to "get good enough for God's forgiveness"—is a blessed relief. Accepting God's forgiveness is an easy act. It is an act of humble receiving, not an act of earning or achieving.

What the Word Says	What the Word Says to Me
For all have sinned and fall short of the glory of God. (Rom. 3:23)	------------------------------ ------------------------------
If we say that we have fellowship with Him, and walk in darkness, we lie and do not practice the truth. . . . If we say that we have no sin, we deceive ourselves, and the truth is not in us. (1 John 1:6, 8)	------------------------------ ------------------------------ ------------------------------ ------------------------------ ------------------------------

For by grace you have been saved
through faith, and that not of
yourselves; it is the gift of God,
not of works, lest anyone should
boast. (Eph. 2:8–9)

No Sin Too Great

So many people seem to be locked into this lie that Satan has fed to their spirits: You have done something so terrible that it is beyond God's forgiveness. God's Word declares that no person is beyond God's love and forgiveness, regardless of what they have done!

We only need to take a brief look at the Word of God to see that, among others, God forgave

- *Abraham and Sarah,* who missed God's perfect plan for their lives, the result being a child that Abraham should not have caused to be born;
- *Moses,* who committed murder;
- *David,* who committed adultery;
- *Peter,* who denied knowing Jesus three times, in the time of Jesus' greatest suffering;
- *Paul,* who persecuted Christians and was responsible for the death of Christians.

God had a plan for the redemption and complete reconciliation of each of these great leaders in the Bible. His plan for redemption through Jesus Christ is offered to all today, regardless of the nature or magnitude of their past sins.

One of the teachings about sin in the New Testament is that all sin is equal before God. In other words, there are no bad sins, not-so-bad sins, and only-a-little-bad sins. Sin doesn't exist by degree. Sin is sin. A person either has a sin nature or doesn't have a sin nature. Sin stains the spirit regardless of its "type" or "size."

God's offer of forgiveness covers *all* sin. No variety or dimension of sin is beyond His loving capacity for forgiveness.

What the Word Says	What the Word Says to Me
Blessed are those whose lawless deeds are forgiven, And whose sins are covered; Blessed is the man to whom the LORD shall not impute sin. (Rom. 4:7–8)	_____ _____ _____ _____ _____ _____
Do not be deceived. Neither fornicators, nor idolaters, nor adulterers, nor homosexuals, nor sodomites, nor thieves, nor covetors, nor drunkards, nor revilers, nor extortioners will inherit the kingdom of God. And such were some of you. But you were washed, but you were sanctified, but you were justified in the name of the Lord Jesus and by the Spirit of our God. (1 Cor. 6:9–11)	_____ _____ _____ _____ _____ _____ _____ _____ _____ _____ _____ _____

- *What new insights do you have into God's power to forgive all manner of sin?*

_____

_____

God's Mercy Cannot Be Exhausted

Another group of people seem to believe that they have exhausted God's mercy through repeated sinful acts after their salvation. Satan has fed them the lie: "You have known God's forgiveness, and now look, you are sinning again. God's fed up with you. He's not going to continue to forgive you time after time."

God's Word says that God has "abundant mercy" (1 Peter 1:3). We cannot exhaust His supply of forgiveness. Each and every time we sin, we are to come to God and ask for His forgiveness, and then by faith, receive His forgiveness and to ask for His help that we might not sin again as we have.

What the Word Says	What the Word Says to Me
The grace of our Lord was exceedingly abundant. (1 Tim. 1:14)	----------------------------------- ----------------------------------- -----------------------------------
The Lord is not slack concerning His promise . . . but is longsuffering toward us. (2 Peter 3:9)	----------------------------------- ----------------------------------- -----------------------------------
He who has begun a good work in you will complete it until the day of Jesus Christ. (Phil. 1:6)	----------------------------------- ----------------------------------- -----------------------------------

What good news to know that we can be forgiven, regardless of our past! If you encounter people who believe they have put themselves outside the realm of God's forgiveness, share the encouraging truth of God: "You can *still* be forgiven! You are not beyond God's ability to forgive you. Your past does not need to be your future."

- *What new insights do you have into forgiveness?*

_____

_____

- *How do you feel about God's promises related to forgiveness?*

_____

_____

- *In what ways are you being challenged in your spirit today regarding forgiveness?*

_____

_____

YOU ARE A CITIZEN OF HEAVEN

You are heaven-bound! That's the encouraging news to every person who has believed in Jesus Christ and received God's forgiveness. Jesus said, "For God so loved the world that He gave His only begotten Son, *that whoever believes in Him should not perish but have everlasting life*" (John 3:16, emphasis mine). A person gains two things the instant he accepts Christ into his life: eternal life, and an everlasting heavenly home.

Throughout the New Testament we have numerous references to our heavenly home and to eternal life. Even so, a significant number of Christians struggle and are discouraged about their spiritual state and about their future. They question whether they are truly saved. They wonder if they will go to heaven when they die.

In this lesson, we will deal first with our assurance of salvation and the gift of everlasting in heaven. Then, we will deal with how we are to live daily "in the hope of heaven."

The Assurance of Eternal Life and a Heavenly Home

Those who believe that they somehow can "lose" their salvation once they have believed in Jesus Christ tend also to be those who believe that they had something to do with gaining their salvation in the first place. The fact is, you did absolutely *nothing* to warrant your salvation—to earn it, achieve it, or to be worthy of it. Your salvation was a gift of God, extended to you by His mercy and out of His fathomless love and made possible for you to receive through the shed blood of Jesus Christ on the cross. The initiative for your salvation was God's. It was God through His Spirit who convicted you of your sin and wooed you to Christ Jesus. It is God who saved you and then filled you with His Holy Spirit. It is God who promised you eternal life. And it is God who will bring you to the fullness of a life with Him in heaven.

The Bible refers to Jesus not only as the "author" of your faith, but also the "finisher" of your faith (Heb. 12:2). The good work He has started in you, He is committed to completing! (1 Thess. 5:24).

In like manner, there is absolutely *nothing* you can do to "undo" your salvation. Just as a baby cannot return to the womb and its life as a fetus after it has been birthed, so you cannot return to your old sin nature once you have been born again spiritually. Your nature has been changed.

Romans 10:9–10 tells us,

> If you confess with your mouth the Lord Jesus and believe in your heart that God has raised Him from the dead, you will be saved. For with the heart one believes unto right-eousness, and with the mouth confession is made unto salvation.

If you have any doubt today about your salvation, go to God, own up to your sinful nature that has separated you from Him, believe in what Jesus did for you on the cross—dying for your sins so that you might live eternally—and confess your faith in Jesus Christ to God. Receive His forgiveness. And then believe with your faith that you, indeed, are saved! You are a child of God forever, fully reconciled and justified before Him.

Be encouraged as you remind yourself of the following passages from God's Word.

What the Word Says	What the Word Says to Me
For I am not ashamed of the gospel of Christ, for it is the power of God to salvation for everyone	_____ _____ _____ _____

who believes. (Rom. 1:16)

He who believes in the Son has everlasting life. (John 3:36)

Jesus, the author and finisher of our faith. (Heb. 12:2)

Now may the God of peace Himself sanctify you completely; and may your whole spirit, soul, and body be preserved blameless at the coming of our Lord Jesus Christ. He who calls you is faithful, who also will do it. (1 Thess. 5:23–24)

But now having been set free from sin . . . you have your fruit to holiness, and the end, everlasting life. For the wages of sin is death, but the gift of God is eternal life in Christ Jesus our Lord. (Rom. 6:22–23)

For he who sows to the Spirit will of the Spirit reap everlasting life. (Gal. 6:8)

Absent from the Flesh, Present with the Lord

The understanding of the apostles was clear: Death is not an end point for the believer but merely a transition into the direct presence of the Lord. Paul wrote to the Corinthians that "to be absent from the body" is to be "present with the Lord" (2 Cor. 5:6–8).

Paul also described death to the Corinthians merely as a "change" (1 Cor. 15:52–54). We move in a moment's time from living in a temporary fleshly home called our physical body on a physical earth to living in a glorified body in our eternal home, heaven (1 Cor. 15:42–44).

What the Word Says	What the Word Says to Me
We are always confident, knowing that while we are at home in the body we are absent from the Lord. . . . We are confident, yes, well pleased rather to be absent from the body and to be present with the Lord. (2 Cor. 5:6, 8)	--------------------------------- --------------------------------- --------------------------------- --------------------------------- --------------------------------- --------------------------------- ---------------------------------
We shall be changed. For this corruptible must put on incorruption, and this mortal must put on immortality. So when this corruptible has put on incorruption, and this mortal has put on immortality, then shall be brought to pass the saying that is written, "Death is swallowed up in victory." (1 Cor. 15:52–54)	--------------------------------- --------------------------------- --------------------------------- --------------------------------- --------------------------------- --------------------------------- --------------------------------- --------------------------------- ---------------------------------

Our Coming Resurrection

The writers of the New Testament also spoke frequently about our coming resurrection, which is made possible by the resurrection of Jesus Christ. In fact, the writer of Hebrews stated that the "resurrection of the dead" is one of the elementary principles of Christ (Heb. 6:1–2).

Jesus said of Himself, "I am the resurrection and the life. He who believes in Me, though he may die, he shall live. And whoever lives and believes in Me shall never die" (John 11:25–26). The apostle Paul taught that just as we have been crucified with Christ, so we shall be raised from death as Christ was raised (Rom. 6:5, 8–9).

As you read the verses below, be encouraged about the resurrection day that lies ahead for you!

What the Word Says	What the Word Says to Me
For if we have been united together in the likeness of His death, certainly we also shall be in the likeness of His resurrection. . . .	--------------------------------- --------------------------------- --------------------------------- ---------------------------------

Now if we died with Christ, we
believe that we shall also live with
Him, knowing that Christ, having
been raised from the dead, dies no
more. Death no longer has
dominion over Him. (Rom. 6:5,
8–9)

But now Christ is risen from the
dead, and has become the first-
fruits of those who have fallen
asleep. For since by man came
death, by Man also came the resurrection of the dead. For as in
Adam all die, even so in Christ all
shall be made alive. (1 Cor.
15:20–22)

Promises to the Overcomer

Those who stay true to Jesus Christ and follow Him to the best
of their ability will be those whom the Holy Spirit helps to overcome sin and evil. And what a promise lies ahead for those who
overcome! John cited a number of these:

- to eat from the tree of life (Rev. 2:7)
- to receive the crown of life (Rev. 2:10)
- to be clothed in white garments (Rev. 3:5)
- to receive a new name, and the name of God and the
  city of God (Rev. 3:12)
- to sit with Jesus on His throne (Rev. 3:21)

Our eternal life will be a life marked by rewards and everlasting blessings.

- *In what ways are you feeling challenged or encouraged in your
  spirit?*

Our Heavenly Home

Jesus wanted His disciples to be assured that they would have a heavenly home. He comforted them by saying,

> Let not your heart be troubled; you believe in God, believe also in Me. In My Father's house are many mansions; if it were not so, I would have told you. I go to prepare a place for you. And if I go and prepare a place for you, I will come again and receive you to Myself; that where I am there you may be also. And where I go you know, and the way you know. . . . I am the way, the truth, and the life. No one comes to the Father except through Me. (John 14:1–4, 6)

Jesus not only is preparing a heavenly home for us, but He has provided the means for us to enter into that home. As sure as our salvation is the surety of heaven!

And what a glorious place our heavenly home is going to be! John described it as a place where all things will be made new and where there will be no more sorrow, suffering, or pain. We will live in the everlasting presence of God (Rev. 21:3–5).

Heaven is a place where we are going to be totally known, and where we will have a complete understanding of God, ourselves, and our relationship with Him. It will be a place where there is no doubt, no confusion, no misunderstanding, no estrangement, and no miscommunication (1 Cor. 13:12)!

As you read the verses below, be encouraged about the home that will one day be yours . . . forever!

What the Word Says	What the Word Says to Me
For now we see in a mirror, dimly, but then face to face. Now I know in part, but then I shall know just as I also am known. (1 Cor. 13:12)	------------------------------
God Himself will be with them and be their God. And God will wipe away every tear from their eyes; there shall be no more death,	------------------------------

nor sorrow, nor crying. There shall
be no more pain, for the former
things have passed away. . . .
"Behold, I make all things new."
(Rev. 21:3b–5)

They shall see His face, and His
name shall be on their foreheads.
There shall be no night there:
They need no lamp nor light of
the sun, for the Lord God gives
them light. And they shall reign
forever and ever. (Rev. 22:4–5)

(Read all of Revelation 21 and 22 for a wonderful preview of heaven.)

God has a wonderful future planned for the true believer in Christ Jesus. It is a future that shouldn't be missed! Those who are elderly and those who are seriously ill are among those who *especially* need to hear the encouraging word of eternal life and a heavenly home. Be quick to share God's Word with all who are suffering or who may be near death.

- *What new insights do you have into God's assurance of your eternal life and home?*

- *How do you feel when you think about heaven and living with God forever?*

- *In what ways are you feeling challenged and encouraged in your own spirit? Is the Lord leading you to share this message of encouragement with a specific person?*

Living in the Hope of Heaven

We are challenged repeatedly in God's Word to live "in the hope of heaven." Heaven is to be at the forefront of our thinking. It is to be our constant hope and anticipation, an active and lively hope in us.

This hope works in three ways in us:

1. We have a renewed desire to abstain from evil and pursue righteousness, as well as a new appreciation for all things eternal.
2. We have a new desire to witness to others about Christ Jesus.
3. We experience great joy about the future.

A Focus on the Eternal

The person who has his eyes on a heavenly home and heavenly rewards is a person who is going to want to do everything within his power to abstain from evil and embrace what God calls good. There is a new focus or concentration on the things of God and a stripping away from anything that might detract.

Along with this new alignment of priorities, the person with an active hope of heaven has a renewed energy and enthusiasm for all things that are eternal. There is a new ability to see that some trials and troubles in this life are only for a "little while." In the context of eternity, many things suddenly appear trivial or momentary.

There is also a renewed interest in the Word of God, which endures forever, and in associating with those who believe in the Word of God.

What the Word Says	What the Word Says to Me
Therefore we also, since we are surrounded by so great a cloud of witnesses, let us lay aside every weight, and the sin which so easily ensnares us, and let us run with endurance the race that is set before us. (Heb. 12:1)	_____ _____ _____ _____ _____ _____ _____

Blessed be the God and Father of
our Lord Jesus Christ, who according to His abundant mercy has
begotten us again to a living hope
through the resurrection of Jesus
Christ from the dead, to an inheritance incorruptible and undefiled
and that does not fade away,
reserved in heaven for you, who are
kept by the power of God through
faith for salvation ready to be
revealed in the last time. In this you
greatly rejoice, though now, for a
little while, if need be, you have
been grieved by various trials, that
the genuineness of your faith, being
much more precious than gold that
perishes, though it is tested by fire,
may be found to praise, honor, and
glory at the revelation of Jesus
Christ. (1 Peter 1:3–7)

All flesh is as grass,
And the glory of man as the
flower of the grass.
The grass withers,
And its flower falls away,
But the Word of the LORD endures
forever. (1 Peter 1:24–25)

Therefore, since all these things
will be dissolved, what manner of
persons ought you to be in holy
conduct and godliness, looking for
and hastening the coming of the
day of God. . . . We, according to
His promise, look for new heavens
and a new earth in which righteousness dwells. Therefore,
beloved, looking forward to these

things, be diligent to be found by
Him in peace, without spot and
blameless. (2 Peter 3:11–12,
13–14)

_____

_____

_____

_____

A Desire to Witness About Christ

The person who has a living, active hope about heaven is a person who will want to produce as much eternal "fruit" as possible, especially the winning of lost souls. The person who truly believes in a glorious future heavenly home will want as many people as possible to enter heaven with him!

What the Word Says	What the Word Says to Me
The fruit of the righteous is a tree of life, And he who wins souls is wise. (Prov. 11:30)	_____ _____ _____ _____
Go therefore and make disciples of all the nations, baptizing them in the name of the Father and of the Son and of the Holy Spirit, teaching them to observe all things that I have commanded you. (Matt. 28:19–20)	_____ _____ _____ _____ _____ _____

Joy About the Future

The person who has an active, living hope about heaven has an exuberance of joy. There is a delight in knowing that God is at work and that we shall one day experience the fullness of His work in us. There is a joy in _knowing_ that we will _always_ have a tomorrow in which to love and serve our Creator!

• _In what ways are you feeling challenged or encouraged in your spirit?_

_____

_____

LESSON 5

GOD IS IN CONTROL

One of the most encouraging verses in the entire Bible, and a verse that most Christians know by memory, is Romans 8:28:

> And we know that all things work together for good to those who love God, to those who are the called according to His purpose.

This verse assures us that God is involved in every moment of our lives and that He is always at work to bring about His good and eternal purposes for us.

The question nearly always arises, however, "If a good God is involved in all things, why do bad things happen?"

Why does a spouse abandon a marriage? Why does a child use drugs? Why does a person lose a job? Why does a family experience a financial setback? Why does a person experience a major, life-threatening disease?

We each can feel discouraged if we dwell on the negative. Ultimately, we may begin to think, "What difference does it make if I follow God?"

Let me say three things as we begin this lesson:

1. *God is involved in* all *things*. He simply can't be separated from any aspect of life since He is the creator, sustainer, and orchestrator of all that is. He is actively involved in all details of His creation.

2. *God has given man free will.* You have been made in the image of God, and part of His image is that you have freedom of choice. It is out of mankind's freedom of choice that Adam and Eve sinned. The result of their sin is that all of us are born with a capacity *and* a propensity to choose sin. We have an inbred sin nature.

Much of the evil that occurs in our world today is rooted in our free will. A spouse *chooses* to abandon the marriage. The child *chooses* drugs. The company *chooses* to lay off employees.

Sometimes our choices are made unconsciously. A person may not choose to bring on a life-threatening disease, but years and years of choosing to live in certain ways with certain habits sometimes results in disease. A person may not choose indebtedness or financial setback, but years and years of overextending or of not saving may result in a financial crisis. The cause of many problems, including many diseases, is still unknown to us. We live in a degree of ignorance, and invariably we will make some bad choices in our ignorance.

In still other instances, the "choices" that govern our lives are collective ones over which we have no personal control. We live in a world that is polluted, crime-ridden, and in many areas, war-torn. The fault lies with no one person and is not the result of one, singular choice. The collective "whole" of mankind's free will has simply gone amok, and individuals are victims of a fallen world.

God will not override free will. Most people have a "stay-out-of-my-life-until-I-need-you" attitude toward God. He does not impose.

This does not mean that God is absent. In the midst of our bad choices—willful, unwillful, individual, or collective—God is present. He is *with* us in our times of trouble, doubt, and struggle. He is always at work on our behalf, desiring our ultimate and eternal best. His Holy Spirit will continue to woo us to an acceptance of Christ and an opening of our heart to God's love.

Furthermore, we must recognize that sin has consequences. When we come to God, accept the sacrifice of Jesus Christ on the cross, and receive God's forgiveness, we receive four things:

1. *We receive a cleansing of our hearts*—a freedom from the guilt and shame we have known in the past.

2. *We receive a "new nature"*—we are freed from our old sin nature and are given the new nature of Christ Jesus from that moment on.
3. *We receive the gift of the Holy Spirit* who works in us to enable us to live a new life that is in keeping with our new nature.
4. *We receive the assurance that we have eternal life.*

God does not promise us, however, that we will not reap from what we sowed into our lives prior to our coming to Him for forgiveness. He may *choose* to avert those consequences, but He does not *promise* us that He will do so. What He does promise is that He will use all things for our good and that He will prepare us to spend eternity with Him.

God does not override our free will or negate the choices that we make with our free will.

> • *Can you recall an experience in which you chose to do something that you knew was apart from God's commandments? What happened?*

_____

_____

3. *God's ultimate purposes* will *be accomplished.* In the end, God will have His way. His will *will* be done.

None of us is capable of seeing the big picture of God's plan because it extends into eternity. God alone knows what He has planned and how He intends to accomplish His master plan. Of one thing we can be certain, God will remain omnipotent, omniscient, and omnipresent. His nature will not change.

He will always have the *power* to do what He desires to accomplish.

He will always *know* precisely what to do to accomplish His purposes.

He will always have sufficient *time* to accomplish His purposes.

We may rebel against God's purposes, balk at His laws, disobey His commandments, and stubbornly refuse His forgiveness. Nevertheless, what God has planned, God will do. The decision that we face is this: Will we get in line with God's plan, or will we rebel against it?

What the Word Says	What the Word Says to Me
I know that You can do everything, And that no purpose of Yours can be withheld from You. (Job 42:2)	
I am Almighty God; walk before Me and be blameless. And I will make my covenant between Me and you. (Gen. 17:1b–2)	
Great and marvelous are Your works, Lord God Almighty! Just and true are Your ways, O King of the saints! Who shall not fear You, O Lord, and glorify Your name? For You alone are holy. (Rev. 15:3–4)	
Now it shall come to pass, if you diligently obey the voice of the LORD your God, to observe carefully all His commandments . . . that the LORD your God will set you high above all nations of the earth. And all these blessings shall come upon you and overtake you, because you obey the voice of the LORD your God. . . . But it shall come to pass, if you do not obey the voice of the LORD your God . . . that all these curses will come	

upon you and overtake you.
(Deut. 28:1–2, 15)

`---------------------------------`
`---------------------------------`

Our Response to God Determines Our Outcome

The response we each must make continually in our lives is this: *I choose to yield the control of my life fully to God.*

All to God, Nothing Withheld

Yielding control to God is a response we must make with regard to every area of our lives; we must not withhold anything. We must yield control of our time, our energy, our talents, our money and other resources, our dreams, our desires, our future, and our total selves. Our surrender to Him must be a complete surrender. God is in *all* things and His purposes will ultimately be accomplished, but He will only take control of all areas of our individual, personal lives if we ask Him to do so.

Two people cannot hold the wheel of an automobile without something going awry on their journey. One alone must be the driver. The same is true in our lives. We must give control to God and invite Him to be the driving force and direction of our lives.

The Bible refers to this yielding of control as submission (James 4:7). It is regarded as a "sacrifice" of self to God (Rom. 12:1).

What the Word Says	What the Word Says to Me
Submit to God. . . . Draw near to God and He will draw near to you. Cleanse your hands, you sinners; and purify your hearts, you double-minded. . . . Humble yourselves in the sight of the Lord, and He will lift you up. (James 4:7–8, 10)	------------------------------- ------------------------------- ------------------------------- ------------------------------- ------------------------------- ------------------------------- -------------------------------
I beseech you therefore, brethren, by the mercies of God, that you present your bodies a living sacrifice, holy, acceptable to God,	------------------------------- ------------------------------- ------------------------------- -------------------------------

which is your reasonable service.
(Rom. 12:1)

_____

_____

* _How do you feel about God's call to submit your life totally to Him?_

_____

_____

* _In what ways are you feeling challenged in your spirit today?_

_____

_____

Consult God *Always*

A person who has totally yielded his or her life to Christ Jesus will be a person who consults God about His will

* at all times,
* about all things, and
* in all situations, circumstances, and relationships.

God is in control of the ongoing daily details of our lives only to the extent that we ask Him often, "What do You want me to do?"

No situation, circumstance, or relationship is beyond God's caring. He desires to impart to us His wisdom, answers, and solutions.

Yielding to God is not something we do only once at the time we are saved. It is something we do continually for the rest of our lives. It is an active *consulting* of God in all things.

What the Word Says	What the Word Says to Me
The LORD is with you while you are with Him. If you seek Him, He will be found by you. (2 Chron. 15:2)	_____ _____ _____ _____
Seek the LORD while He may be found, Call upon Him while He is near. (Is. 55:6)	_____ _____ _____

O God, You are my God;
Early will I seek You;
My soul thirsts for You;
My flesh longs for You
In a dry and thirsty land.
(Ps. 63:1)

Trust God in Methods and Timing

God does not always manifest "control" *when* or *how* we think He should. God, however, knows precisely which method to use in which circumstance. He knows what is best for each life. And He knows precisely when to employ His chosen method. Our role is to trust Him implicitly.

God speaks to each of us in a voice we can understand. He acts in each of our lives in a way that causes us to confront our lives and to see Him clearly. When it comes to our own individual lives, God will always impart His will to us in ways that we can comprehend. We can know His timing and His methods *for us*.

In the broader scope of life, however, we are not always told what methods God is going to use. We do not know what God will choose to do to convict a lost sinner of his sin. We do not know what God will do to soften a hardened heart or to alter a rebellious course. We are to adopt a position of trust: God knows, and God will act when and how He chooses to act. His purposes are always for good, and so are His methods and His timing.

Jesus said of His second coming that even He did not know God's precise timing: "But of that day and hour no one knows, no, not even the angels of heaven, but My Father only" (Matt. 24:36).

Even when we know with a certainty in our spirits that God is in control and that God is going to act, we must always wait for God to do so *in His timing*. If God reveals to us what He is going to do, it is so that we might be ready to respond when He acts— not so that we can jump ahead of God and exact His justice or extend His mercy prior to His chosen timetable. We err greatly anytime we get ahead of God or attempt to take matters of justice into our own hands.

In yielding control to God, our prayer must always be, "Not my will, but Yours. Not my method, but Yours. Not my timing, but Yours."

We must also recognize at all times that God is not only concerned about us individually, but about all of His children. He acts in ways that are beneficial to each of His beloved ones. Sometimes the will of God is delayed so that more souls may be saved, or even so that one particular lost sheep may be found.

As we trust God to act in the lives of others, we are to have a spirit of expectancy. We are to *look* for God at work, and we are to praise Him equally for His long-suffering, His execution of judgment, and His granting of mercy.

What the Word Says	What the Word Says to Me
Read Job 38–39.	
You are God, Ready to pardon, Gracious and merciful, Slow to anger, Abundant in kindness. (Neh. 9:17b)	
The LORD is righteous in all His ways, Gracious in all His works. The LORD is near to all who call upon Him, To all who call upon Him in truth. (Ps. 145:17–18)	

• *How do you feel about our call to trust God in methods and timing? Do you feel encouraged that the Lord is slow to wrath and patient in judgment? Do you feel encouraged that His methods are not always mankind's methods?*

_____

_____

The Encouraging Word

Some of the most encouraging statements you can ever share with another person are these:

- God is in control of the situation, and He will accomplish His purposes.
- You can put yourself on God's side—the side of victory.
- You can trust God to act in precisely the right timing and with precisely the right method to accomplish the ultimate good in any situation, and in any life.

This world is under the influence of the devil, but it is not under his control. God is in control—now and always.

Pause for a few moments to reflect upon the awesome power of God, and then answer these questions:

- *What new insights do you have into God's control over all things? Over your life?*

_____

_____

- *Have you yielded full control for your life to God? Are you trusting God to exert control on a daily basis in your life?*

_____

_____

- *How are you being challenged in your role as one of God's encouragers? Is the Lord directing you to share the encouraging word that "God is in control" with a specific person? What is His timing for you to sharing that message of encouragement? What is God's method for you to use in sharing this message of encouragement?*

_____

_____

LESSON 6

GOD WILL
ENABLE YOU

For many Christians, life is a matter of simply doing the best they can. They experience no dynamic, no power, and no sense of victory in their souls. A humdrum spiritual life leads to discouragement. A spiritual life without a sense of progress, growth, and development can become tedious and wearisome.

Such a life, however, is *not* what God desires for us. The Bible holds out the *promise* of the Holy Spirit, who indwells us to enable us, equip us, and help us to lead an abundant, vibrant, purposeful life.

The Promise of the Spirit

Jesus promised His disciples, "I will not leave you as orphans; I will come to you" (John 14:18 NASB). He further promised, "I tell you the truth, it is to your advantage that I go away; for if I do not go away, the Helper shall not come to you; but if I go, I will send Him to you" (John 16:7 NASB).

Just before His ascension into heaven, Jesus said, "You shall be baptized with the Holy Spirit not many days from now . . . you shall receive power when the Holy Spirit has come upon you" (Acts 1:5, 8 NASB).

The promise of the Holy Spirit is for all who believe. Time and again in the New Testament, those who confessed Jesus as Lord were filled with the Holy Spirit. The presence of the Holy Spirit is made available to all. Just as in salvation—in which a person receives the forgiveness of God *by faith*—so, too, receiving the Holy Spirit is an act of faith.

- *In your life, have you experienced the joy of being filled with the Holy Spirit?*

_____

_____

A Constant and Lasting Presence

The Holy Spirit dwells with us. He does not "come and go," but rather, He resides within our spirits on a permanent basis.

The frequent image used by the writers of the New Testament is that we are a temple of God, filled with the Spirit of God.

What the Word Says	What the Word Says to Me
If the Spirit of Him who raised Jesus from the dead dwells in you, He who raised Christ from the dead will also give life to your mortal bodies through His Spirit who dwells in you. (Rom. 8:11)	
Do you not know that you are the temple of God and that the Spirit of God dwells in you? . . . The temple of God is holy, which temple you are. (1 Cor. 3:16–17)	
Hold fast the pattern of sound words which you have heard from me, in faith and love which are in Christ Jesus. That good thing which was committed to you, keep by the Holy Spirit who dwells in us. (2 Tim. 1:13–14)	

• *What insights do you have into the abiding nature of the Holy Spirit within us?*

_____

_____

The Work of the Holy Spirit in Us

The Holy Spirit operates within us on a daily, ongoing basis to help us in all practical matters of Christian living. Specifically, the Holy Spirit works in the following ways:

• *Convicts us of sin* and makes us aware when we are breaking God's commandments (John 16:8–11).
• *Illuminates the Word of God to us,* helping us to understand and apply what we read in the Bible (John 16:12–15).
• *Teaches us the truth about God,* the truth about ourselves, and the truth about the relationship God desires to have with us (John 16:12–15).
• *Guides us into right decisions and choices* and into right avenues of service and ministry (Rom. 8:14).
• *Assures us that we are born again and are the children of God,* and, thus, are heirs with Christ of all God's promises and blessings (Rom. 8:16).
• *Frees us from the bondage of fear* (Rom. 8:15).
• *Intercedes on our behalf,* always praying the will of God for us (Rom. 8:26).
• *Warns us,* so that we might put on the whole armor of God and engage successfully in spiritual warfare (Acts 20:23).

In our daily battle against the temptations of this world, the Holy Spirit prompts us continually about what is right and wrong. We do not have the role model of Jesus on the earth today to be a living picture for us about how to live; the Holy Spirit reveals to us the right way. The Holy Spirit also equips us to fight and defeat the enemy of our souls. He assures us that we have victory over an already-judged, already-defeated foe (John 16:11).

What a Helper the Holy Spirit is to us! His presence in us is active constantly. He is always seeking our highest and best good, now and for all eternity.

What the Word Says

[Jesus said]: "When He [the Holy Spirit] has come, He will convict the world of sin, and of righteousness, and of judgment; of sin, because they do not believe in Me; of righteousness, because I go to My Father and you will see Me no more; of judgment, because the ruler of this world is judged." (John 16:8–11)

[Jesus said]: "I still have many things to say to you, but you cannot bear them now. However, when He, the Spirit of truth has come, He will guide you into all truth; for He will not speak on His own authority, but whatever He hears He will speak; and He will tell you things to come. He will glorify Me, for He will take of what is Mine and declare it to you. All things that the Father has are Mine. Therefore I said that He will take of Mine and declare it to you." (John 16:12–15)

For as many as are led by the Spirit of God, these are sons of God. (Rom. 8:14)

For you did not receive the spirit of bondage again to fear, but you

What the Word Says to Me

received the Spirit of adoption by whom we cry out, "Abba, Father." (Rom. 8:15)

The Spirit Himself bears witness with our spirit that we are children of God, and if children, then heirs—heirs of God and joint heirs with Christ, if indeed we suffer with Him, that we may also be glorified together. (Rom. 8:16–17)

Likewise the Spirit also helps in our weaknesses. For we do not know what we should pray for as we ought, but the Spirit Himself makes intercession for us with groanings which cannot be uttered. Now He who searches the hearts knows what the mind of the Spirit is, because He makes intercession for the saints according to the will of God. (Rom. 8:26–27)

Now I go bound in the spirit to Jerusalem, not knowing the things that will happen to me there, except that the Holy Spirit testifies in every city, saying that chains and tribulations await me. (Acts 20:22–23)

• *Reflect upon your life and recall several specific ways in which the Holy Spirit has helped you.*

• *In what ways are you being challenged to trust the Holy Spirit for His help?*

_____

_____

Creation of Our New Identity

The Holy Spirit works within us to create a new "character" or identity in us. Our new nature is marked by these characteristics (Gal. 5:22-23):

- *Love*—for those who do not love in return.
- *Joy*—even in the midst of painful circumstances.
- *Peace*—when something we were counting on doesn't come through.
- *Long-suffering*—when things aren't going fast enough for us.
- *Kindness*—toward those who treat us unkindly or have rejected us.
- *Goodness*—toward those who have been intentionally insensitive to us or have sought to do us harm.
- *Faithfulness*—when friends have proved unfaithful.
- *Gentleness*—toward those who deal harshly with us and persecute us for no just cause.
- *Self-control*—in the face of intense temptation.

Conversely, the Holy Spirit strips away from us the old characteristics we exhibited before we received God's Spirit—chiseling at us bit by bit, sanding away our sinful habits and the hard edges of our personalities. He causes us to put away our former behaviors—deeds that Paul calls "works of the flesh" and which he describes as behaviors such as "adultery, fornication, uncleanness, licentiousness, idolatry, sorcery, hatred, contentions, jealousies, outbursts of wrath, selfish ambitions, dissensions, heresies, envy, murders, drunkenness, revelries, and the like" (Gal. 5:19–21a).

The new character traits that the Holy Spirit produces in us are called the "fruit" of the Holy Spirit. They are the very character traits that marked Jesus' life! Indeed, the Holy Spirit is "Christ in

us." The apostle Paul wrote to the Galatians, "I have been crucified with Christ; it is no longer I who live, but Christ lives in me;
and the life which I now live in the flesh I live by faith in the Son
of God, who loved me and gave Himself for me" (Gal. 2:20).

• *How do you feel when you think about the Holy Spirit residing
within you to change you into the likeness of Christ Jesus?*

_____

_____

Ability to Stand Against the Devil

The Holy Spirit's presence in us gives us the ability to say "no"
to the devil's temptations and lies and also the ability to withstand
the devil's assaults on our life.

What the Word Says	What the Word Says to Me
Likewise you also, reckon your-selves to be dead indeed to sin, but alive to God in Christ Jesus our Lord. Therefore do not let sin reign in your mortal body, that you should obey it in its lusts. And do not present your members as instruments of unrighteousness to sin, but present yourselves to God as being alive from the dead, and your members as instruments of righteousness to God. (Rom. 6:11–13)	
Now having been set free from sin, and having become slaves of God, you have your fruit to holi-ness. (Rom. 6:22)	
Be strong in the Lord and in the power of His might. Put on the whole armor of God, that you may be able to stand against the	

wiles of the devil. . . . Take the hel-
met of salvation, and the sword of
the Spirit, which is the word of
God; praying always with all
prayer and supplication in the
Spirit, being watchful to this end
with all perseverance and supplication. (Eph. 6:10–11, 17–18)

Ability to Witness About Christ Jesus

The first and foremost sign of the Holy Spirit's presence in a person's life is the power to give witness to Christ Jesus (Acts 1:8). We each are called to present Christ to others—in our words as well as our deeds.

What the Word Says	What the Word Says to Me
[Jesus said]: "Let your light so shine before men, that they may see your good works and glorify your Father in Heaven." (Matt. 5:16)	
[Jesus said]: "You shall receive power when the Holy Spirit has come upon you; and you shall be witnesses to Me in Jerusalem, and in all Judea and Samaria, and to the end of the earth." (Acts 1:8)	

• *In what ways are you feeling challenged in your spirit today?*

Our Daily Walk in the Spirit

God calls us to "walk in the Spirit" (Gal. 5:16, 25). We do this when we ask the Holy Spirit daily for guidance in all that we do: at the time of each major decision we make, in the face of each new problem we encounter, in the course of each conversation we have. We must learn to listen to the voice of the Spirit speaking in us. As we do, the Holy Spirit becomes an ever-present source of encouragement to us.

The person who knows that . . .

- he has the assurance of eternal life
- he cannot fail if he obeys God's commands
- he will receive the full provision and protection of the Holy Spirit until his mission in life is fulfilled

. . . is a person who is able to live in boldness and joy.

The Holy Spirit is the Encourager who lives within. He is the Enabler of the abundant life Jesus promised us when He said, "The thief does not come except to steal, and to kill, and to destroy. I have come that they may have life, and that they may have it more abundantly" (John 10:10).

- *What new insights do you have into the encouraging role that the Holy Spirit can have in our lives?*

_____

_____

- *In what ways are you feeling challenged to share the message of the Holy Spirit as Encourager and Enabler? Is the Lord dealing with you to speak to a specific person?*

_____

_____

YOU CAN LIVE IN FREEDOM

Freedom! What a wonderful word to us. We all value freedom highly. We delight in being free. We long to live in freedom always.

One of the most encouraging and recurring themes in the New Testament is that Christians are free in Christ Jesus. This especially was good news to the Christians who first received this teaching from the apostles since many of the first believers throughout the Roman Empire were officially classified as slaves. The freedom that the apostles spoke about, however, was not a political freedom but, rather, a spiritual one. They spoke of an inner freedom that allows a person to live above his present circumstances.

This is a freedom that is no less important in our world today, when many people feel trapped in the bondage of addictions, depression, abusive relationships, and other oppressive situations. The world in which we live is not a godly world, and we each must experience the freedom that Christ offers to us so that we can live in the world, yet not be "of" the world.

To any person who feels as if he or she is in the clutches of something negative or evil, the encouraging word is, "You can be free!"

The Foundation of Our Freedom

Our freedom in Christ is directly related to two main concepts in the Bible:

1. *Redemption*—we have been redeemed by Christ Jesus.
2. *Service*—we each are destined as human beings to serve one of two masters.

The choice to receive Christ brings about our redemption and puts us into the service of God. A failure to receive Christ keeps a person from experiencing redemption and keeps the person in servitude to the "law of sin and death."

Redemption

The word *redemption* in the Greek and Roman culture literally referred to the purchase of a slave from the marketplace, with the purpose of giving the slave his freedom. In spiritual terms, the word means that the blood of Jesus paid the "ransom" that was required for each of us to be set free from our sin nature and experience the fullness of God's forgiveness and love. God provided a total means of redemption through the death of Jesus on the cross. Revelation 5:9 tells us about Jesus, "You were slain, / And have redeemed us to God by Your blood / Out of every tribe and tongue and people and nation."

Jesus taught His disciples that His very purpose was to provide redemption. He said, "The Son of Man did not come to be served, but to serve, and to give His life a ransom for many" (Matt. 20:28, Mark 10:45). Paul also referred to the redemptive purpose of Jesus when he wrote, "There is one God and one Mediator between God and men, the Man Christ Jesus, who gave Himself a ransom for all" (1 Tim. 2:5–6a).

Redemption is not a concept limited to the New Testament. The message of redemption can be seen from cover to cover in the Bible: God planned for our redemption (Gen. 1–2); God required redemption (Gen. 3:11); God prepared the way for redemption (Gen. 12–Mal.); God instituted His redemptive plan through Jesus Christ (the Gospels); news of God's redemptive plan was spread (Acts); the redemptive plan was explained (the Epistles); and the redemption of man will be consummated (Rev.). The entire Bible is the story of God's redeeming love.

Your spiritual freedom and mine has been purchased for us by God through His Son Jesus Christ. Just as no slave could redeem himself, so no person can redeem himself spiritually. We are indebted forever to the One who paid the price for our freedom, since there is no means by which we can pay Him back for what He has done for us.

Therefore, although we are free from sin, we are not really free to do solely as we please. We have a great debt of gratitude; indeed, we "owe" our eternal lives to Christ Jesus, who purchased our freedom for us.

Service

A second important concept related to our freedom is this: As human beings, we *will* serve one of two masters; we either will serve God and His system of righteousness or we will serve the devil and his system of evil. Romans 6:18 says, "Having been set free from sin, you became slaves of righteousness." Jesus said that no man can serve two masters simultaneously. We will serve either one or the other.

The Nature of Our Freedom

When we put these two concepts together, we come to the conclusion that while we have been set free from the bondage of sin and death, we are set free to *serve* God in righteousness. Our freedom is not unlimited, unbridled freedom. Salvation is never a license to sin. Rather, our freedom is the freedom that allows us the great privilege to live above the world's systems and the law of sin and death. We no longer are enslaved to sinful passions, lusts, and desires. Instead, we are the bondservants of Christ.

As you read through the verses below, consider especially these questions:

- *How do you feel about God's provision for you?*

_____

_____

- *How do you feel about God's claim upon your life?*

_____

_____

• *In reflecting upon your own life, in what areas do you have a need today to experience God's redemptive freedom?*

_____

_____

What the Word Says

What the Word Says to Me

He has delivered us from the power of darkness and translated us into the kingdom of the Son of His love, in whom we have redemption through His blood, the forgiveness of sins. (Col. 1:13–14)

You were not redeemed with corruptible things, like silver or gold, from your aimless conduct received by tradition from your fathers, but with the precious blood of Christ, as of a lamb without blemish and without spot. (1 Peter 1:18–19)

Do you not know that to whom you present yourselves slaves to obey, you are that one's slaves whom you obey, whether of sin to death, or of obedience to righteousness? But God be thanked that though you were slaves of sin, yet you obeyed from the heart . . . and having been set free from sin, you became slaves of righteousness. . . . For just as you presented your members as slaves of uncleanness, and of lawlessness leading to more lawlessness, so now present your members as slaves of righteousness for holiness. (Rom. 6:16–19)

No one can serve two masters; for
either he will hate the one and
love the other, or else he will be
loyal to the one and despise the
other. (Matt. 6:24)

Whatever you do, do it heartily, as
to the Lord and not to men,
knowing that from the Lord you
will receive the reward of the
inheritance; for you serve the
Lord Christ. (Col. 3:23–24)

Freedom from Evil

The freedom we experience from the law of sin and death is manifested in one of these three ways:

1. We are set free from recurring temptation.
2. We experience deliverance from evil power.
3. We receive grace to trust God.

Each of these manifestations of freedom may be experienced in different times and situations.

Freedom from Temptation

No person is ever entirely free from temptation, but we can experience a release from a "season" or a siege of temptation. We see this in the life of Jesus when He was in the wilderness being tempted by the devil. The tempter came to Jesus with three rounds of temptation, and each time, Jesus refuted him with the Word of God. In the final round, Jesus commanded the devil, "Away with you, Satan! For it is written, 'You shall worship the LORD your God, and Him only you shall serve'" (Matt. 4:10). At that, the Bible tells us, "the devil left Him, and behold, angels came and ministered to Him" (v. 11). There was a definitive end to this season of temptation in Jesus' life.

This does not mean that Jesus was never tempted again. Rather, it means that Jesus functioned in full freedom as He conducted His ministry of preaching, teaching, and healing. The issue of His loyalty to God alone had been settled in a definitive way, and Jesus could never again be tempted on that point.

Each of us has a propensity to sin in certain ways. The devil knows that, and it is at our weakest point that he comes to tempt us—sometimes in a way that seems unrelenting. How can we experience freedom from his steady barrage of temptation? By using the same method that Jesus used: We can speak the Word of God every time the tempter whispers his lies to us. For example:

- When the devil tells us that we are weak, we can declare, "God says I am strong" (Joel 3:10).
- When the devil says that we are doomed to failure, we can declare, "God says that I am more than a conqueror" (Rom. 8:37).
- When the devil says that we can never change, we can declare, "God says that I am a new creature in Christ Jesus" (2 Cor. 5:17).
- When the devil says that we are not worthy of God's love, we can declare, "God says that He loved me so much He sent Jesus to die for my sins so that I might live with God forever!" (John 3:16).

Regardless of what temptation to sin you may experience, God has provided a passage of His Word that declares such a temptation to be a lie of Satan intended for your harm. Find the portion of God's Word that applies to your specific circumstance and use it as a "sword of the Spirit" (Eph. 6:17).

- *In your life, is there a temptation that seems to reoccur with some regularity or frequency? What does God's Word say about this temptation?*

_____

_____

The Role of Prayer. When faced with recurring temptation, we must also ask for the help of the Holy Spirit in withstanding the temptation. Jesus said that when we pray, we are to pray, "Do not lead us into temptation"—in other words, do not allow us to get into situations in which we are subject to the devil's tempting (Matt. 6:13). On the night in which Jesus was betrayed in the Garden of Gethsemane, He had said to His disciples, "Watch and pray, lest you enter into temptation. The spirit indeed is willing, but the flesh is weak" (Matt. 26:41). We are not only to speak God's Word to the tempter, but to ask God for strength *not* to yield to the devil's temptations.

All Are Tempted. Many people seem to be discouraged at the fact that they still experience temptation after they are born again. The fact is, all people are tempted, for all of their lives. We are never beyond temptation.

We must be very clear on two points, however: 1) God does not tempt us to do evil just to see if we will yield. God has no association whatsoever with evil. 2) The Holy Spirit can help us withstand evil. We must never attempt to justify our behavior by saying, "The devil made me do it" or "God made me this weak so He knows I couldn't help myself." The Holy Spirit is our strong ally in helping us withstand temptation. We can resist the devil and his lies. And the good news is that when we resist the devil, he *will* flee from us (James 4:7).

What the Word Says	What the Word Says to Me
Blessed is the man who endures temptation; for when he has been proved, he will receive the crown of life which the Lord has promised to those who love Him. Let no one say when he is tempted, "I am tempted by God;" for God cannot be tempted by evil, nor does He Himself tempt anyone. But each one is tempted when he is drawn	_____ _____ _____ _____ _____ _____ _____ _____ _____ _____ _____

away by his own desires and
enticed. (James 1:12–14)

Resist the devil and he will flee
from you. (James 4:7)

Deliverance

In some cases, as discussed above, God asks us to use our will, to use His Word, and to rely upon the Holy Spirit to withstand temptation. In other cases, God chooses sovereignly to deliver us from evil and to wipe out the evil force that is coming against us.

Moses experienced this at the crossing of the Red Sea. As he and the children of Israel were camped by the Red Sea and the enemy armies of Pharaoh were approaching rapidly to take the Israelites back into slavery, the Lord gave these words to Moses:

> "Do not be afraid. Stand still, and see the salvation of the LORD, which He will accomplish for you today. For the Egyptians whom you see today, you shall see again no more forever. The LORD will fight for you, and you shall hold your peace" (Ex. 14:13–14).

That is precisely what came to pass. The Lord opened up the Red Sea before Moses so that all the children of Israel could walk across on dry ground, and then when the armies of Pharaoh were crossing behind them, the Lord closed the waters, and the entire army was destroyed. "Not so much as one of them remained" (Ex. 14:28b).

God completely delivered the Israelites from this enemy. They still faced other enemies and other challenges, but Pharaoh and his army never came against them again.

Jesus had an active ministry of deliverance to those who were possessed or oppressed by the devil. Time and again, He rebuked the evil spirits that kept men, women, and children in bondage. The spirits fled at His command and did not return. The deliverance was definitive and complete.

If you know a person who is in need of deliverance from an evil spirit, there are five things they and you must do:

1. *Do not be afraid.* God tells us plainly that the Holy Spirit in us is greater than the devil of this world (1 John 4:4).
2. *Ask other believers to join with you in prayer and fasting.*
3. *Speak against the oppressing spirit in the name of Jesus.* There is no greater power on earth than the Name of Jesus; His name is higher than anything that attempts to rule over us (Phil. 2:9–10).
4. *Believe that God will act on your behalf.* Firmly put your trust in God and believe that when you call upon Him, He hears and answers you (Ps. 91:14–15).
5. *Upon claiming deliverance from a problem by faith, seek immediately to fill the void left behind in the wake of that addiction, problem, or spirit with a "solution."*

If the person's mind has been occupied with thoughts of evil, he must take all thoughts captive and turn his attention to God's Word and fill his mind with thoughts of righteousness. This is done by reading and studying God's Word, but, above all, by memorizing God's Word (2 Cor. 10:4–5).

If the person's time has been spent in sinful activities, he must find something new and *righteous* to do with his time. Time spent pursuing sin can be turned into time spent in prayer or in service to others.

If the person's associates have been themselves associated with evil, he must find new friends, colleagues, or coworkers. He must get involved in a Bible-believing church and stay involved in the church.

To fail to take a positive step forward is to invite evil to return (Matt. 12:43–45).

What the Word Says	What the Word Says to Me
You are of God, little children, and have overcome them, because He who is in you is greater than he who is in the world. (1 John 4:4)	_____ _____ _____ _____ _____
Therefore God also has highly	_____

exalted Him and given Him the
name which is above every name,
that at the name of Jesus every
knee should bow, of those in
heaven, and of those on earth, and
of those under the earth. (Phil.
2:9–10)

If the Son makes you free, you
shall be free indeed. (John 8:36)

Because he has set his love upon
Me, therefore I will deliver him;
I will set him on high, because he
has known My name.
He shall call upon Me, and I will
answer him;
I will be with him in trouble;
I will deliver him and honor him.
With long life I will satisfy him,
And show him My salvation. (Ps.
91:14–16)

For the weapons of our warfare
are not carnal but mighty in God
for pulling down strongholds,
casting down arguments and
every high thing that exalts itself
against the knowledge of God,
bringing every thought into captivity to the obedience of Christ.
(2 Cor. 10:4–5)

Trust in God's Grace

At still other times, the Lord provides freedom for us *not* by bringing an end to a season of temptation or sovereignly delivering us
from evil, but by giving us more of His grace to withstand the trial.
Paul experienced this. Three times Paul prayed and asked God
to free him from what he called a "thorn in the flesh" that had been
given to him as a "messenger of Satan." Rather than remove this

thorn, however, the Lord said to Paul, "My grace is sufficient for you, for My strength is made perfect in weakness" (2 Cor. 12:9a).

God's higher purpose—one of trust, a stronger faith, and a more potent witness—was worked in Paul's life. Paul came to the point where he declared, "I will rather boast in my infirmities, that the power of Christ may rest upon me.... For when I am weak, then I am strong" (2 Cor. 12:9b–10).

Did Paul experience freedom in his spirit? Most definitely. It was not the freedom *from* the thing that plagued him, but it was a freedom to trust God to be sufficient in all things and at all times.

If God does not remove a temptation from you or does not deliver you sovereignly from an evil situation, God may very well be calling upon you to experience a freedom to abide in His presence and to trust Him *in spite of* an evil situation, circumstance, or trial.

The Means Are up to God

We are not in a position to choose which means God might use to bring us into a new dimension of freedom in Christ Jesus. The encouraging news, however, is that the Lord promises us a "way out" of the evil that comes against us. He will not allow us to be tempted beyond our ability to withstand a temptation. He assures our redemption. We will not remain bound or captive to an evil situation, circumstance, addiction, person, or relationship if we turn to Him and ask for His help.

What the Word Says	What the Word Says to Me
No temptation has overtaken you except such as is common to man; but God is faithful, who will not allow you to be tempted beyond what you are able, but with the temptation will also make the way of escape, that you may be able to bear it. (1 Cor. 10:13)	-------------------------------
[Jesus said]: "The one who comes to Me I will by no means cast out." (John 6:37)	-------------------------------

- *In thinking back over your life, reflect on times when God "freed" you from evil by giving you these three gifts:*
  1. *the power to withstand temptation;*
  2. *deliverance from evil;*
  3. *grace to trust God even more.*

_____

_____

- *What new insights do you have into these three means that God uses in providing freedom from evil oppression to those who trust in Him?*

_____

_____

- *In what ways are you feeling challenged to take this encouraging message to others? Is God dealing with you to take this encouragement to a specific person?*

_____

_____

Two Freedoms We Enjoy

As Christians, not only do we enjoy freedom from the oppression of sin and evil, but we enjoy these two freedoms:

1. Freedom to fully know our purpose in living and to fulfill that purpose;
2. Freedom to serve.

These are freedoms we must claim by our faith and pursue. They do not happen to us automatically, but they are ours for the asking.

Freedom to Fulfill Our Purpose

God has made each of us with unique talents and gifts, which are to be used for a unique role in furthering His kingdom on earth. We are His workmanship, and He desires for us to know both the talents and the role for which we have been created (Eph. 2:10).

Ask God to reveal to you His purpose for your life. The person who discovers his talents and knows why and how God intends for him to use his talents is a person who is not plagued by self-doubt or low self-esteem. There is great freedom in knowing that you are valuable and important to God and that He is guiding your steps and preparing you for even greater blessings.

The encouraging word is that God has a design for your life. He has a means for you to experience great satisfaction and fulfillment.

What the Word Says	What the Word Says to Me
For we are His workmanship, created in Christ Jesus for good works, which God prepared beforehand that we should walk in them. (Eph. 2:10)	------------------------------
God saw everything that He had made, and indeed it was very good. (Gen. 1:31)	------------------------------

• *In your life are you experiencing the freedom that comes from knowing who God created you to be and what He has called you to do?*

_____

_____

• *In what ways are you feeling challenged or encouraged today?*

_____

_____

Freedom to Serve Others

When we know who we are in Christ Jesus—the redemption that we have experienced in our salvation, the talents we have been given, the role we are to fill—we then experience a great freedom to serve others. We lose our self-conscious pride. We are willing to take risks in showing love to others. We know we are saved, we know who we are, and we know we are called to be God's people on the earth!

The person who has his identity clearly in focus is a person who has very few emotional or spiritual barriers. He feels utterly free to speak *whatever* God leads him to speak, to do *whatever* God leads him to do, and to go *wherever* God leads.

The encouraging news is that God has work for you to do! He has someone who needs what you have to give. He has a purpose for you, and He wants you to be fulfilled in life.

What the Word Says	What the Word Says to Me
[Jesus said]: "As you go, preach, saying, 'The kingdom of heaven is at hand.' Heal the sick, cleanse the lepers, raise the dead, cast out demons. Freely you have received, freely give." (Matt. 10:7–8)	_____ _____ _____ _____ _____ _____
For you, brethren, have been called to liberty; only do not use liberty as an opportunity for the flesh, but through love serve one another. (Gal. 5:13)	_____ _____ _____ _____

• *In your life, are you experiencing the freedom to serve others?*

_____

_____

• *In what ways are you being challenged or encouraged in your spirit today?*

_____

_____

• *In what ways is the Lord dealing with you to take this message of encouragement to others?*

_____

_____

LESSON 8

YOU ARE BEING TRANSFORMED

Every Christian is in the process of being changed, more and more, into the nature of Christ Jesus.

Now there are many books on the market today about self-improvement; they almost universally advocate that a person can change himself into the person he wants to be. While intellectual and emotional growth and development are certainly possible in the natural realm, *spiritual change* does not happen at the will of man.

A person who seeks to change himself spiritually is a person who believes that if he can just do more good deeds, learn more about God, or accomplish more for God's kingdom, he will be a "better" person. This approach inevitably results in anxiety, frustration, discouragement, feelings of failure, and perhaps even depression.

The encouraging news of the Bible is that you cannot change yourself spiritually, but *God is in the process of changing you!* From the moment you accept Jesus Christ as your Savior and receive God's forgiveness, you enter God's "change" process. Your spiritual transformation occurs at the initiative of God, and according to His timetable and methods.

The Bible tells us that we are being transformed in two ways:

1. We are being transformed by the renewal of our minds.
2. We are being conformed into the image of Christ.

In each case, the Holy Spirit is the "agent of the change" that occurs within us. We have a part to play, but the Holy Spirit is the One who causes the change to take place within us.

You will not be the person in the future that you are today if you submit yourself to God's transformation process. You are going to be more like Jesus. And that's good news!

* *How do you feel about personal spiritual change?*

_____

_____

Transformed in Attitude

The transformation of your mind is a transformation from the way the world thinks to the way God thinks. Paul wrote to the Romans:

I beseech you therefore, brethren, by the mercies of God, that you present your bodies a living sacrifice, holy, acceptable to God, which is your reasonable service. And do not be conformed to this world, but be transformed by the renewing of your mind, that you may prove what is that good and acceptable and perfect will of God. (Rom. 12:1–2)

The two points of view—God's and man's—are nearly always opposite. Let me give you just a few examples:

The world tells you to get even with your enemies. God says to leave vengeance up to Him and to love your enemies, do good to them, and pray for them (Matt. 5:43–44, Rom. 12:19–21).

The world tells you to fight for your rights and defend yourself at all costs. God says to turn the other cheek (Matt. 5:38–39).

The world tells you that hard work and education will result in success. God says that faith and learning to listen to His voice and obey Him are what bring a person to success (Heb. 11).

As Christians, we are called to think like God thinks, and then, with our renewed minds, to act as Jesus would act if He walked in our shoes on the earth today. A difference in thinking results in a difference in living.

What the Word Says	What the Word Says to Me
This I say, therefore, and testify in the Lord, that you should no longer walk as the rest of the Gentiles walk, in the futility of their mind, having their understanding darkened, being alienated from the life of God, because of the ignorance that is in them, because of the hardening of their heart; who, being past feeling, have given themselves over to licentiousness, to work all uncleanness with greediness. But you have not so learned Christ . . . as the truth is in Jesus: that you put off, concerning your former conduct, the old man which grows corrupt according to the deceitful lusts, and be renewed in the spirit of your mind, and that you put on the new man which was created according to God, in righteousness and true holiness. (Eph. 4:17–24)	_____

The Word Renews Our Thinking

How is it that we experience a renewal of the mind so that we can think as Jesus thought? We acquire a renewed mind through a habit of reading God's Word frequently and regularly. Ephesians 5:26 refers to a cleansing by the "washing of water by the word." The more we read God's Word and trust the Holy Spirit to quicken what we read to our spirits, the more the Word acts to cleanse our thoughts so that we think the pure thoughts of Christ.

The more we read God's Word, the more we are confronted with God's truth. The Word of God convicts us of error and points out to us the need for change. It presents to us the truth and compels us to act on the truth.

The more we read God's Word, the more we become familiar with "God's opinion" and the more the Holy Spirit makes His opinion our opinion. The Word of God becomes *the way we think*. And when that happens, we experience a genuine change. We begin to speak differently, act differently, make wiser choices, and adopt new priorities. Our lives take on a new nature that flows from our new mind.

(I especially encourage you to read Proverbs in the Old Testament and the Gospels and Epistles in the New Testament. These books are filled with practical wisdom that can readily be applied to daily life.)

What the Word Says	What the Word Says to Me
Be diligent to present yourself approved to God, a worker who does not need to be ashamed, rightly dividing the word of truth. But shun profane and vain babblings, for they will increase to more ungodliness. And their message will spread like cancer. (2 Tim. 2:15–17)	_____
For the word of God is living and powerful, and sharper than any two-edged sword, piercing even to the division of soul and spirit, and of joints and marrow, and is a discerner of the thoughts and intents of the heart. (Heb. 4:12)	_____
You must also put off all these: anger, wrath, malice, blasphemy, filthy language out of your mouth. Do not lie to one another, since you have put off the old man with his deeds, and have put on the	_____

new man who is renewed in
knowledge according to the image
of Him who created him. (Col.
3:8–10)

Do not hide Your commandments
from me.
My soul breaks with longing
For Your judgments at all times.
You rebuke the proud—the
cursed,
Who stray from Your command-
ments.
Remove from me reproach and
contempt,
For I have kept Your testimonies. . . .
Your testimonies also are my
delight
And my counselors. (Ps.
119:19–22, 24)

- *Reflect upon your life. How has your thinking changed since you
  became a Christian? How has reading the Word of God brought
  about change in your life?*

We Can Choose What We Think

The mind is subject to the will. We each have control over what
we *choose* to think about. Paul wrote to the Corinthians that they
should be engaged in "bringing every thought into captivity to
the obedience of Christ" (2 Cor. 10:5). We have the ability to
screen, select, admit, and cultivate what goes into our minds. We
can keep our minds from wandering into evil thoughts by choosing to focus our minds, instead, upon what is good in God's eyes
(Phil. 4:8).

We also have the ability to choose *how* we will think about what
we perceive with our senses. While we have no control over some

things that come into our field of vision or within our range of hearing as we live our daily lives, we *do* have control over what we will think about what we perceive or sense, and how we will act on that information.

For example, David *saw* Bathsheba. He wasn't looking for her. He was out walking on his balcony one night and while surveying the city below him, he saw a beautiful woman bathing. That could have been the end of the story. David could have turned and walked back into his palace and thought nothing more about what he had seen.

Instead, David began to *think* about what he saw. He "sent and inquired about the woman." He did some research, he began to dwell in his mind on what it would be like to get a closer look at her and what it might be like to be with her. Eventually he sent for her, sinned with her, and suffered serious consequences for that sin (2 Sam. 11:2–4).

When things come into our range of sensation or perception, we immediately are to evaluate them with the "filter" of God's Word. If we find ourselves dwelling on a thought, we must ask ourselves, "Why am I thinking this? What is at the root of my thought? What will happen if I continue to think this way? Is that really the direction I want my life to go?" We do not need to act out of impulses, desires, and lusts. We can govern what we *choose* to think and then *choose* to do.

What the Word Says	What the Word Says to Me
Whatever things are true, whatever things are noble, whatever things are just, whatever things are pure, whatever things are lovely, whatever things are of good report, if there is any virtue and if there is anything praiseworthy—meditate on these things. (Philippians 4:8)	_____ _____ _____ _____ _____ _____ _____ _____ _____ _____

• *In what ways are you feeling challenged or encouraged in your spirit?*

_____

_____

God's Truth Planted in Our Memories

What we put into our minds is what we have in our "memory bank." Jesus said that one of the ways the Holy Spirit helps us is by bringing to our remembrance what Jesus said (John 14:26).

When we commit the Word of God to memory or even read God's Word repeatedly and frequently as a life habit, the Holy Spirit can then bring God's Word quickly to our minds when we are making a decision or facing a problem. His "answer" becomes the thought that drives our actions. In this way, the Holy Spirit effects change within us. No longer are we limited only to our own intellect, emotions, and memories of what we have learned and experienced—our lives have a new foundation of God's Word on which to make right choices.

What the Word Says

[Jesus said]: "But the Helper, the Holy Spirit, whom the Father will send in My name, He will teach you all things, and bring to your remembrance all things that I said to you." (John 14:26)

My son, if you receive my words,
And treasure my commands within you,
So that you incline your ear to wisdom,
And apply your heart to understanding;
Yes, if you cry out for discernment,
And lift up your voice for understanding,

What the Word Says to Me

_____

_____

_____

_____

_____

_____

_____

_____

_____

_____

_____

_____

_____

If you seek her as silver,
And search for her as for hidden
treasures;
Then you will understand the fear
of the LORD,
And find the knowledge of God.
For the LORD gives wisdom.
From His mouth come knowledge
and understanding. (Prov. 2:1–6)

Many people are discouraged today because they are confused, plagued by recurring negative thoughts, or because they don't know which way to turn in their lives. What an encouraging word you can share with them that God can transform their lives by the renewing of their minds! They can experience a real change in their lives, one that begins in the way they think.

- *In what way are you being challenged to share this word of encouragement with others? Is the Lord dealing with you to give this word of encouragement to a specific person?*

Conformed to Christ's Image

The transformation process is one that begins in the mind. The conformation process is one that largely deals with our habits.

God's desire is that we become more and more like Jesus in the things we do, which means that our "automatic responses" to life—our habitual daily rituals and the routine way in which we handle life—must reflect Christ's nature.

Paul wrote to the Romans that God's purpose is that we "be conformed to the image of His Son" (Rom. 8:29). We all know the phrase "Like father, like son." In our case, we are to be "like Father, like Son."

Christ in Us

The conformation process begins with our acknowledgment that Christ dwells within us. His Spirit occupies and fills our spirit. Jesus told His disciples that when the Holy Spirit came, He would dwell within them (John 14:17). Paul wrote repeatedly that the "Spirit of God dwells in you," that we have "the Spirit of Christ," and that "Christ is in you" (Rom. 8:9–10).

Christ is not just "added" to our life, but, rather, His very nature is implanted within us. If anything, the process becomes one of subtraction—there is a sanding, a removal from us of all the old habits and automatic behaviors that are not like Christ.

God chisels away at us, chipping off the old dead patterns of behavior. He often uses painful methods to bring us to the realization that we are *not* acting as Christ would act. Sometimes He uses family members, friends, failures, financial setbacks, or even physical ailments to cause us to face our lives and ask, "What is God trying to strip away from me so that I am more like Jesus?"

What the Word Says

[Jesus said]: "The Spirit of truth, whom the world cannot receive, because it neither sees Him nor knows Him, but you know Him, for He dwells with you and will be in you." (John 14:17)

And we know that all things work together for good to those who love God, to those who are the called according to His purposes. For whom He foreknew, He also predestined to be conformed to the image of His Son, that He might be the firstborn among many brethren. Moreover whom He predestined, these He also called; whom He called, these He also justified; and whom He justified, these He also glorified. (Rom. 8:28–30)

What the Word Says to Me

_____

_____

_____

_____

_____

_____

_____

_____

_____

_____

_____

_____

_____

_____

_____

_____

_____

_____

_____

• *How do you feel when God chips away at those things in your life that are not like Christ?*

Abiding in Christ

God's conformation process is one that is always aimed at bringing us to a greater trust and reliance upon Him. It is always aimed at our submitting our will to His. It is always aimed at our experiencing God's highest and best blessings.

The picture that Jesus used to depict this conformation process was one of a vine and its branches. Jesus said:

> Abide in Me, and I in you. As the branch cannot bear fruit of itself, unless it abides in the vine, neither can you, unless you abide in Me. I am the vine, you are the branches. He who abides in Me, and I in him, bears much fruit; for without Me you can do nothing. . . . If you abide in Me, and My words abide in you, you will ask what you desire, and it shall be done for you. By this My Father is glorified, that you bear much fruit; so you will be My disciples. (John 15:4–5, 7–8)

When you look at a vine, it is virtually impossible to tell where the vine stalk and its branches begin and end. The sap flows through a vine into its branches, pushing out growth and producing fruit. It is a *living* process, not a mechanical one.

What Jesus calls each of us to do is to so abide in Him—to rely solely upon His Holy Spirit to give life to our spirits. Ultimately, as we live in Christ and He lives in us, the Holy Spirit conforms us fully to Christ's nature. Sinning becomes foreign to us; righteousness becomes the norm of our lives (1 John 3:5–6, 5:18).

What exactly is it that is conformed? Our speech and our behaviors. We speak what is true, loving, and right. We do what is righteous, loving, and of most help. We respond to life's circumstances and situations just as Jesus would respond to them.

In a practical way, how do we "abide" in Christ? Jesus said, "If My words abide in you." Again, we must take in the Word of God into our lives so that we fully understand God's commandments, the teachings of Jesus, and the way that God desires for us to live. This goes beyond a frequent reading of God's Word to a real study of God's Word. God's Word abides in us when we seek out the deeper riches of meaning in it—getting answers to our questions, solutions to our problems, and insights into what God has ahead for us. Study takes time. It requires focus. But it is something that is doable for every person. God will always take you at your current level of understanding and, as you read and study His word, move you to a deeper level of understanding.

We also abide in Christ by communicating with God on a continual, continuous basis. Prayer becomes a way of life for us. We are always consulting God in our spirits. We are always mindful of His presence. We are always in a state of thanksgiving and praise and appreciation for what He is doing for us, in us, and through us. We talk to God regularly—in our minds and in our spoken words of praise and petition.

We spend time alone with God, listening for Him to speak to us. We share with Him the innermost secrets and desires of our hearts. We develop a *spiritually intimate* relationship with God.

And the encouraging news is that every Christian believer can do this! Each of us can choose to spend time in the Word, in prayer, and in listening to God.

As you read the verses below, be encouraged that you *are* becoming like Jesus as you abide in Him, study His Word, spend time in prayer, and rely on Him with increasing trust.

What the Word Says	What the Word Says to Me
Behold what manner of love the Father has bestowed on us, that we should be called children of God! . . . Beloved, now we are children of God; and it has not yet been revealed what we shall be, but we know that when He is revealed, we shall be like Him, for we shall see Him as He is. And	_____ _____ _____ _____ _____ _____ _____ _____

everyone who has this hope in Him purifies himself, just as He is pure. (1 John 3:1–3)

And you know that He was manifested to take away our sins, and in Him there is no sin. Whoever abides in Him does not sin. (1 John 3:5–6b)

And this I pray, that your love may abound more and more in knowledge and all discernment, that you may approve the things that are excellent, that you may be sincere and without offense till the day of Christ, being filled with the fruits of righteousness which are by Jesus Christ, to the glory and praise of God. (Phil. 1:9–11)

- *What new insights do you have into God's conformation process?*

_____

_____

- *How do you feel about the fact that God is conforming you into the likeness of Christ Jesus?*

_____

_____

- *In what ways are you being challenged or encouraged in your spirit?*

_____

_____

GOD HAS A WAY THROUGH THE STORM

At no time in the teachings of Jesus do we find a promise to Christians that they are exempt from the struggles, suffering, and storms of life. Rather, what we find is repeated teaching that

- God will be with us in the storms;
- God is greater than any storm;
- God will bring us through the storms of life as we trust in Him (and at times, He will choose to bring us through a storm directly to His presence in heaven); and
- God will always use a storm for our ultimate good—to strengthen us, refine us, and cause good to come our way—if we will trust in Him for *His* purposes to be accomplished in our lives.

At no time, however, are we promised a storm-free life. Our challenge is not to avert or spend our efforts avoiding the inevitable but, rather, to set our spirits to respond to stormy times. Peter wrote this to the early church as it faced Roman persecution:

Gird up the loins of your mind, be sober, and rest your hope fully upon the grace that is to be brought to you at the revelation of Jesus Christ. (1 Peter 1:13)

Peter's advice is not, "Here's how to escape the storm." Rather, he tells these believers who were facing intense times of trial solely because they were Christians, "Here's how to *prepare* for the trouble ahead."

The Nature of Storms

Generally speaking, there are two types of storms: (1) ones that strike us suddenly and without warning, and (2) storms that we see coming, often long in advance of their arrival. Both types of storms come our way. There is no escaping them.

What causes storms? They have three origins.

1. *There are storms that we create.* We often hate to admit this fact, but we cause many of the problems we face in life—sometimes willfully and out of a rebellious spirit, but often innocently and out of ignorance.

2. *There are storms that are created by others.* Now, far fewer storms are created by others than most people claim. We all are prone to self-justification and attempts at blaming others for our problems. Still, there are some storms that legitimately are caused by other people.

3. *There are storms that are created by general circumstances in which no one human being or group of people is at fault.* Natural disasters, general mechanical equipment, and the wearing out or depletion of resources are examples. A flood would be a "storm" that might be considered circumstantial.

- *Identify a storm in your life that had its origin in each of these three areas:*
  1. Self-induced storm:
  2. Storm caused by others:
  3. Circumstantial storm:

_____

_____

• *How did you feel in each of these cases? In general, how does a storm make you feel?*

_____

_____

What God Says About Storms

The Word of God gives us seven important truths about the storms that blow into our lives:

1. Storms come to all people, Christians and non-Christians.
2. Jesus knows all about the storm in your life.
3. God doesn't always deal with the storm in the way we think He will or should.
4. Jesus always offers a word of comfort in the storm.
5. Jesus always issues a command in the midst of the storm.
6. Jesus gives us power to obey His storm-related command.
7. We always come face-to-face with important truths as the result of storms.

Many of these truths can be seen in the story of Jesus and his disciples during a stormy night in Galilee:

> Immediately Jesus made His disciples get into the boat and go before Him to the other side, while He sent the multitudes away. And when He had sent the multitudes away, He went up on the mountain by Himself to pray. Now when evening came, He was alone there. But the boat was now in the middle of the sea, tossed by the waves, for the wind was contrary.

> Now in the fourth watch of the night Jesus went to them, walking on the sea. And when the disciples saw Him walking on the sea, they were troubled, saying, "It is a ghost!" And they cried out for fear.

But immediately Jesus spoke to them, saying, "Be of good cheer! It is I; do not be afraid."

And Peter answered Him and said, "Lord, if it is You, command me to come to You on the water."

So He said, "Come." And when Peter had come down out of the boat, he walked on the water to go to Jesus. But when he saw that the wind was boisterous, he was afraid; and beginning to sink he cried out, saying, "Lord save me!"

And immediately Jesus stretched out His hand and caught him, and said to him, "O you of little faith, why did you doubt?" And when they got into the boat, the wind ceased.

Then those who were in the boat came and worshiped Him, saying, "Truly You are the Son of God." (Matt. 14:22–33)

As we look at the principles of God related to storms, I encourage you to keep this truth at the forefront of your thinking: *How we respond to storms is more important than determining what caused a storm.* We are not called by God to understand *why* storms come our way as much as we are called by God to *respond* to storms in a way that causes us to grow in our trust of God and to witness to others of God's presence in our lives.

Knowing the origin of a storm may be an important clue as to what God desires to teach us from a storm, but it is never the sole lesson God has for us. The greater lesson is always a lesson we discover by looking at what we *do* when storms strike us.

Read the above passage from Matthew 14 again. Consider the *response* of both Jesus and the disciples to this storm.

• *What initial insights do you have into this passage?*

_____

_____

Storms Come to All People

Storms come into the lives of the righteous as well as the unrighteous. Jesus had fed five thousand men and their families during the day that preceded this stormy night. Then Jesus had commanded His disciples to cross the sea while He went aside to spend time alone with His Heavenly Father. The disciples had done nothing wrong. They were not being corrected by God for an error or sin.

You may not have done anything wrong either to cause or contribute to the storm that comes into your life. Some storms are sent by God for purposes other than *correction*. These likely are storms that God allows to come our way or impact us, as opposed to God's sending them. He will use such storms to bring about our *perfection*.

What the Word Says

In this you greatly rejoice, though now for a little while, if need be, you have been grieved by various trials, that the genuineness of your faith, being much more precious than gold that perishes, though it is tested by fire, may be found to praise, honor, and glory at the revelation of Jesus Christ. (1 Peter 1:6–7)

My brethren, count it all joy when you fall into various trials, knowing that the testing of your faith produces patience. But let patience have its perfect work, that you may be perfect and complete, lacking nothing. (James 1:2–4)

We also glory in tribulations, knowing that tribulation produces perseverance; and perseverance, character; and character, hope. Now hope does not disappoint, because the love of God has been poured out in our hearts by the Holy Spirit who was given to us. (Rom. 5:3–5)

What the Word Says to Me

_____
_____
_____
_____
_____
_____
_____
_____
_____

_____
_____
_____
_____
_____
_____

_____
_____
_____
_____
_____
_____
_____

Jesus Knows About the Storm

Jesus knew that His disciples were in a storm. He knows when you are in a storm.

Jesus knew about the storm on the Sea of Galilee "in the natural." The Sea of Galilee is not a large sea. Under normal conditions, a group of men can row a boat across it in a matter of a couple of hours. Wherever Jesus was praying, the storm was also blowing there!

Jesus also knew that this natural storm caused an "inner storm" in the lives of His disciples. He had seen them before during a stormy time. He knew their hearts.

In times of trouble, we often ask, "Lord, where are you? Do you know what's happening to me?" The fact is, Jesus knows *exactly* where you are. He knows *precisely* what is happening to you.

The darkness or howling of a storm do not keep God from seeing you and hearing you. He knows precisely where you hurt, what you fear, and how helpless you feel. He knows all the details of your financial, physical, or relational storm.

And He cares for you. He is concerned for you. He responds to you not out of your need for Him, but out of His vast, everpresent, and unconditional love for you. God doesn't respond to the fact of the storm. He doesn't even respond to you because of your feelings or your need within the storm. He responds to you because He loves you.

What the Word Says	What the Word Says to Me
[Jesus said]: "Are not five sparrows sold for two copper coins? And not one of them is forgotten before God. . . . Do not fear therefore; you are of more value than many sparrows." (Luke 12:6–7)	_____ _____ _____ _____ _____ _____
He [the wicked] has said in his heart, "God has forgotten; He hides His face, He will never see it." . . . But you have seen it, for You	_____ _____ _____ _____

observe trouble and grief. (Ps.
10:11, 14)

God's Methods Are Higher

Jesus doesn't always come to us when and in the ways we think
He should.

The Bible tells us that Jesus sent His disciples away in a boat
and was alone with the Father "when evening came." He did not
come to them on the stormy sea until the "fourth watch," which
is the time from 3:00 AM to 6:00 AM. The disciples no doubt would
have preferred that Jesus come to them the instant the storm
struck them. They certainly would have preferred for Him to
arrive before they were completely worn out from eight or more
hours of rowing! Jesus, however, came to them at precisely the
moment when He knew that His purposes in their lives would be
accomplished.

Indeed, we have no mention in this story that the disciples cried
out to Jesus prior to His arrival or that they had used their faith
in any way during their struggle against the storm's winds and
waves. We need to cry sooner, as opposed to later, when storms
strike. God does not respond to our need (or to the intensity of our
need), but He does respond to our faith.

Furthermore, Jesus came in a way that was totally unexpected
by His disciples. He appeared to them walking on water, something they had never seen before. They were so startled and
frightened by the method Jesus used that they cried out, "It is a
ghost!"

We sometimes miss seeing Jesus in the midst of our troubled
times because we aren't expecting Him to show up in the *way* that
He comes to us. We must recognize always that God's methods and
ways are of His choosing. They are often beyond our ability to
understand them fully or to anticipate them according to rational
means. Our God is a miracle-working God. He reveals His presence, His power, and His solutions to us in amazing, awe-inspiring
ways. We are to look for Him at all times and in all things so that
we don't miss His arrival.

What the Word Says	What the Word Says to Me
"For My thoughts are not your thoughts, Nor are your ways My ways," says the LORD. "For as the heavens are higher than the earth, So are My ways higher than your ways, And My thoughts than your thoughts." (Isa. 55:8–9)	------------------------------
As for me, I will call upon God, And the LORD shall save me. (Ps. 55:16)	------------------------------

A Word of Comfort

Jesus always gives a word of encouragement and comfort to us.

Regardless of the intensity of the storm or how ominous the trouble, Jesus' word to us is always a word of encouragement. His is not an idle word of optimism. Rather, it is a word of power and strength. The encouraging word that *Jesus* speaks to us in the secret place of our heart is a sure reality—it does come to pass!

As the disciples struggled in their storm, the word of Jesus to them was this, "Be of good cheer! It is I; do not be afraid" (Matt. 14:27). Jesus speaks the same message to us: "Be glad. I'm here. Don't be afraid." Regardless of what Jesus may say to you about your storm or about actions you are to take to endure or turn the tide of trouble coming against you, He will *always* assure you of His presence with you.

What the Word Says	What the Word Says to Me
[Jesus said]: "In the world you will have tribulation; but be of good cheer, I have overcome the world." (John 16:33b)	------------------------------
[Jesus said]: "For the Son of Man has come to seek and to save that	------------------------------

which was lost." (Luke 19:10)

[Jesus said]: "Let not your heart
be troubled; you believe in God,
believe also in Me." (John 14:1)

Jesus Gives a Command

Jesus always gives a command in the midst of the storm. He gives
a directive in every storm situation we find in the New Testament.
His command is either to the storm or to us. On one occasion,
Jesus spoke directly to a storm, saying, "Peace, be still!" (Mark
4:39). When Jesus walked to His disciples on a stormy sea, He gave
a command to Peter, "Come!"

In your time of tribulation, you can always be assured that Jesus
is either going to rebuke the trouble (including dealing with a trou-
blemaker), or He is going to call you to do something in the midst
of the trouble that will strengthen, purify, or otherwise change you.
Look for His command!

Our part is this: during stormy times, we must do the following:

- *Turn to God,* putting our eyes squarely on Him and not
  on the storm.
- *Ask God, "What do You want me to do?* Ask, "Am I to use
  my faith against this storm? Am I to grow in trust by
  riding out this storm?"
- *Do what God tells you to do.* The acid test of faith is always
  obedience. It is not enough to hear God's command
  in the storm. We must obey His command.

What the Word Says	What the Word Says to Me
Read Mark 4:35-38.	
Then He arose and rebuked the wind, and said to the sea, "Peace, be still!" And the wind ceased and there was a great calm. But He said to them, "Why are you so fearful? How is it that you have no	

faith?" And they feared exceed-
ingly, and said to one another,
"Who can this be, that even the
wind and the sea obey Him!"
(Mark 4:39–41)

I will instruct you and teach you
in the way you should go;
I will guide you with My eye. (Ps.
32:8)

Power to Obey

The Holy Spirit empowers and equips us to carry out God's
commands. He gives us the courage, the strength, and the ability
we need to act in obedience.

Jesus said to Peter, "Come!" And then He granted to Peter the
ability to walk on water to Him. Peter did not have that ability in
himself. He had never walked on water before, and we have no evi-
dence that he walked on water after that night. Peter was enabled
to walk on water in direct response to Jesus' command.

Do not hesitate to obey what God tells you to do in the midst of
your trouble or trial. He will enable you to carry out His command.

If He tells you to endure in patience . . . He will give you the
strength to endure in patience.

If He tells you to speak to your storm with faith . . . He will make
your faith effective in calming the storm.

Whatever God commands you to do, He will equip you to do.
Your part is to obey.

What the Word Says	What the Word Says to Me
Then Zerubbabel the son of Shealtiel, and Joshua the son of Jehozadak, the high priest, with all the remnant of the people, obeyed the voice of the LORD their God. . . . Then Haggai, the LORD's messenger, spoke the LORD's message to the people, saying, "I am with	

you, says the LORD." (Haggai
1:12–13)

This is what I commanded them,
saying, "Obey My voice, and I will
be your God, and you shall be My
people. And walk in all the ways
that I have commanded you, that
it may be well with you." (Jer.
7:23)

Discovery in Storms

It is in storms that we often discover the most important truths of our lives.

I can guarantee you that Peter never forgot the night that he walked on water. He also never forgot what he learned from Jesus that night:

- Jesus was preparing him for his future.
- Jesus was revealing His absolute power over all things.
- Jesus was building up his faith.
- Jesus was bringing him to the point where, along with the other disciples, he would say, "Truly You are the Son of God."

I do not know all of the lessons God may teach you as you experience storms, trials, tribulations, and difficulties in your life. I do not know the precise lessons that you will encounter in pain, suffering, and trouble. I do know this: God will always reveal to you something about Himself that will build you up in your inner person and prepare you for greater days ahead.

His lesson to you will be uniquely *for you*. The lesson someone else experiences out of the same storm may not be the lesson that God is giving to you. Look for what He is speaking to your heart and what He is doing in your life.

Most importantly, don't miss out on the lesson that God has for you in the storm. Don't just ride out the storm and then forget what has happened to you. God has a purpose in every storm, and one of those purposes is to change some aspect of your life so that you become more like Jesus.

What the Word Says	What the Word Says to Me
Show me Your ways, O LORD; Teach me Your paths. (Ps. 25:4)	------------------------------- -------------------------------
The LORD looks from heaven; He sees all the sons of men. . . . He fashions their hearts individually. (Ps. 33:13, 15a)	------------------------------- ------------------------------- ------------------------------- -------------------------------

Our Response to Storms

God's desire for us is that we turn to Him during a time of trouble and keep our eyes focused squarely on Him. We are to continue to praise Him and to thank Him for His faithfulness to us. In all things, we are to give God praise and honor and glory.

Many people who are hit with trouble respond in one of these ways:

- *Ignore God.* They turn all of their attention to the trial or storm and never think to consult God
- *Blame God.* They never consider the full purposes of God in the storm or even the origin of the storm
- *Rebel against God.* They often take the attitude, Why serve God if this is what happens?

The Christian is called to do just the opposite: We are to turn to God the instant that trouble hits, ask God to reveal all that He desires to reveal about the origin, nature, and response we are to have against the storm, and trust God to bring about His good purposes in our lives both during and as the result of the storm.

Praise God regardless. He is at work in storms and in fair-weather times!

What the Word Says	What the Word Says to Me
Therefore do not be unwise, but understand	------------------------------- -------------------------------

what the will of the Lord is. . . . Be
filled with the Spirit, speaking to
one another in psalms and hymns
and spiritual songs, singing and
making melody in your heart to
the Lord, giving thanks always for
all things to God the Father in the
name of our Lord Jesus Christ.
(Eph. 5:17–20)

I will greatly praise the LORD with
my mouth;
Yes, I will praise Him among the
multitude. (Ps. 109:30)

Take a few minutes to reflect upon a storm you are currently
experiencing or one that you know another person is experiencing. Then respond to these questions:

- *What new insights from God's Word do you have about a
  storm you may be experiencing?*

  _____

  _____

- *In what ways do you believe God is seeking to encourage
  you by these passages from His Word that you have studied?*

  _____

  _____

- *In what ways are you being challenged to encourage others?
  Is there a specific person to whom the Lord is directing you
  to give this word of encouragement—perhaps someone going
  through a stormy time?*

  _____

  _____

LESSON 10

GOD WILL GIVE YOU HIS ANSWER

All of us have questions. We must never be ashamed of having questions or honest doubts. Our questions are the starting point of every person's search for truth, meaning, and fulfillment in life.

The two broad and general questions that every mature person asks at some point are well known:

- *Who am I?*
- *Why am I here?*

These questions are what I call *identity* questions. They are at the very core of our humanity. We want to know our nature and the purpose for our creation.

Three other questions are ones that tend to relate to specific circumstances, questions, or problems. I call them *situational* questions:

- *What is going on?*
- *Why is this happening?* (This question might also be stated, *What is the meaning of this?*)
- *What should I do?*

The encouraging news is that God not only has answers to each of these questions, but He delights in sharing His answers with us.

Identity Questions

When we ask the questions "Who am I?" and "Why am I here?" we are really asking two other questions, although we may not be aware that we are asking them. Those two questions are, "Who is God?" and "What is God doing?" The answers to our foremost two identity questions are answered to a great extent when we answer these questions about God's identity.

The Bible tells us that God is Creator. "In the beginning, God created" (Gen. 1:1). He created the heavens and the earth and all that is in them—including us. He is our Maker, our Source, our Author.

Who are you? You are a creation of God, uniquely gifted and designed by Him for a specific role and function on this earth.

Consider these words: Creator, Maker, Source, Author. Creator of what? Maker of what? Source of what? Author of what? These very words imply that God has a plan and a purpose for this world and for each person He creates.

A creator creates a place and creatures to occupy it.

A maker makes things happen; he sets in motion functions and processes.

A source provides all that is necessary for a purpose to be accomplished.

An author writes a message that conveys meaning and instructions, as well as words of inspiration or commands to be true to that meaning and carry out the instructions.

If you truly desire to know who you are and why you are here, the Bible presents the answers to you.

You are one of God's creations, unique in all ways and fashioned very specifically for a purpose God has in mind.

You are put into this world to make something happen—you have been created for a specific function in God's plan. The Holy Spirit has been given to you to help you carry out your function. All around you, God is engineering the situations and circumstances necessary for you to fulfill your function as you obey Him.

On a daily basis, God is giving to you all that you need to carry out His plan for you. Not only has God given you your unique set of talents and traits, but He is providing for you life, energy, time, opportunity, and abundant resources to carry out your function.

You are a "living letter" being written by God to your generation with the express intent of communicating to the world God's love and forgiveness. You are a living testimony to the redemption work of Jesus Christ. When you choose to obey God's call upon your life, you become a living example of God's Word at work in the world today.

- *Reflect upon your life:*
  1. How has God gifted you as His unique creation?

  _____

  _____

  2. How has God revealed to you your function or role in His greater plan for all mankind? (What is it that you do well when you use the gifts He has given to you? What has God called you to do?)

  _____

  _____

  3. How has God provided for you, so that you might carry out His plan?

  _____

  _____

  4. How has God challenged you repeatedly to live in obedience to Him, and to express His love and forgiveness to others?

  _____

  _____

- *How do you feel about the identity that God has given to you?*

  _____

  _____

What the Word Says	What the Word Says to Me
Creator: Then God said, "Let Us make	_____

man in Our image, according to
Our likeness: let them have
dominion over the fish of the sea,
over the birds of the air, and over
the cattle, over all the earth and
over every creeping thing that
creeps on the earth."
So God created man in His own
image; in the image of God He
created him: male and female He
created them. Then God blessed
them, and God said to them, "Be
fruitful and multiply; fill the earth
and subdue it; have dominion
over the fish of the sea, over the
birds of the air, and over every living thing that moves on the
earth." (Gen. 1:26–28)

Maker:
It is God who arms me with
strength,
And makes my way perfect.
He makes my feet like the feet of
deer,
And He sets me on my high
places. (Ps. 18:32–33)

He who has begun a good work in
you will complete it until the day
of Jesus Christ. (Phil. 1:6)

Source:
Every good gift and every perfect
gift is from above, and comes
down from the Father of lights.
(James 1:17)

Give us this day our daily bread.
(Matt. 6:11)

Author:
Looking unto Jesus, the author and finisher of our faith. (Heb. 12:2)

And as we have borne the image of the man of dust [Adam], we shall also bear the image of the heavenly Man [Jesus Christ]. (1 Cor. 15:49)

The Psalmist wrote: "I will praise You, for I am fearfully and wonderfully made" (Ps. 139:14). When we truly catch a glimpse of who we are and why we are here—from God's perspective—our automatic response is praise to God. What an awesome God He is! How wonderful we are as His creation! What a perfect plan He has in mind! What an incredible role He has entrusted to us!

- *What new insights do you have into the reason God has placed you on the earth at this time? How does this relate to your role as an encourager?*

- *In what ways are you feeling challenged and encouraged today?*

Situational Questions

When we ask the questions, "What is going on? Why is this happening? What should I do?" we must always ask them in relationship to God's plan and purposes for us:

- What is *God* doing?
- What does *God* intend to happen in and through this event or situation?
- How does *God* want me to respond?

Again, our answers to these questions are to be found in God's Word. As we read God's Word, we can trust the Holy Spirit to quicken God's answers to our spirit so that we know with certainty what God desires for us to know and to respond as God wants us to respond.

Does God truly want to reveal answers to us? The Bible tells us that God desires for us to have His wisdom. James 1:5 6 assures us:

> If any of you lacks wisdom, let him ask of God, who gives to all liberally and without reproach, and it will be given to him. But let him ask in faith, with no doubting, for he who doubts is like a wave of the sea driven and tossed by the wind.

James tells us three important things about our search for God's answers:

1. *We are to ask in faith.* We must believe that when we ask for wisdom from God that He will give it to us. We must accept the answer that we believe we have heard from God and act on it. If we second-guess what we believe God is saying to us, James says that we are going to be "tossed" about and we will be unstable in our actions (James 1:6–8).

As you go to God for answers, *expect* God to give you answers. Have an open heart ready to receive His answers as you study the Scriptures and listen to the Holy Spirit in your heart.

2. *God will give us wisdom liberally.* In other words, He will give us the fullness of the answer that we need to have. He will not keep a secret from us when we need His wisdom to live out His plan and purpose for us to its fullest.

Now, this does not mean that God will tell us everything we *want* to know. It means to us that God will tell us everything we *need* to know from His perspective. Some things will always remain a mystery to us because there simply is no way that we, as finite creatures, can ever comprehend the fullness of God's majesty—His omnipotence, His omniscience, His glory. There are many things we cannot understand about God's nature. They are too awesome for our minds and hearts to contain.

There are other things that we may want to know in our curiosity, but they are things that we do not need to know. The information may actually be harmful to us. In some cases, if God were to impart the information to us we might be tempted to use the information to bring harm to other people, or we might respond to the information in a way that would hurt another person unintentionally.

In still other cases, God does not reveal information to us because it is not yet His timing for us to have that information.

The broader message, however, is this: God always tells us what we *need* to know in order to live out His commandments, be a witness to Christ Jesus, and fulfill His specific role and function for our lives. He keeps no secrets regarding His statutes, the nature of Christ, or the purpose He has for us to be agents of God's love and forgiveness. He always tells us what we need to know to do the work that He has created for us to do. Trust God to give you such information *liberally*.

The fact is, God reveals through His Word far more than most of us can apply! We each know more about what God desires us to do than we either want to do or believe we can do. As God gives us His wisdom, in liberal, overflowing, abundant doses, we must always ask Him to give us the ability, the desire, and the courage to respond with *actions* to the truth of His message to us.

3. *God does not criticize us for asking.* God gives us His wisdom "without reproach." He does not chide us for doubting. He does not ridicule us for not knowing already.

Many people find it very encouraging to realize that God never considers any question too small or any problem too insignificant for God. He is not only the God of eternal and everlasting truth, but He is the God of factual details. You should feel free to ask God *any* question that you have in your heart about your life, your current situation or circumstances, the meaning of what is happening in you, to you, or through you, and the next steps that God desires for you to take.

- *Recall an incident in your life when you believe God gave you His wisdom. How did you feel? What did you do in response?*

- *How do you feel about the truth that God never criticizes those who ask Him honest questions? How do you feel about His promise to give you His wisdom generously?*

What the Word Says	What the Word Says to Me
"He will teach us His ways, And we shall walk in His paths." (Isa. 2:3b)	
Be diligent to present yourself approved to God, a worker who does not need to be ashamed, rightly dividing the word of truth. But shun profane and vain babblings, for they will increase to more ungodliness. (2 Tim. 2:15–16)	
All Scripture is given by inspiration of God, and is profitable for doctrine, for reproof, for correction, for instruction in righteousness. (2 Tim. 3:16)	

Searching the Scriptures for Specific Answers

When you are faced with a situation that baffles you or a problem that continues to puzzle you, spend some concentrated time in God's Word. Use a concordance and identify several key concepts that you believe are related to your problem or question. Then read the Scriptures that are listed under that topic. Make notes to yourself about the meaning you see in each verse or passage you read.

Before you begin reading the Scriptures, invite the Holy Spirit to speak to your heart as you read. Open yourself to hearing His voice speak in your innermost being. He usually speaks to us through strong impressions, sudden new ideas or insights, and through ideas and concepts that we just can't seem to shake after we have finished our study time.

In the course of your reading and studying the Scriptures on a particular topic, other concepts may come to mind, or you may have questions about specific words or phrases that you encounter. Spend some time searching the Scriptures on those topics. The Holy Spirit may also remind you of a passage of Scripture that you have read or studied at a previous time. Follow His lead in your study.

Give yourself several hours—perhaps even several days or weeks—to search the Scriptures before you come to a conclusion about God's answer to you. Now, in some cases, you may find your answer in the first verse you study, or the solution may be quickened to your spirit in the first passage to which you turn. More likely, the truth of God's response to you is to be found as you read and study "precept upon precept, / Line upon line . . . / Here a little, there a little" (Isa. 28:10).

Keep in mind always that God will never give you a directive that is not confirmed in His Word. He will not tell you to do something that is contrary to His commandments, to the life of Jesus Christ, or to the teachings of the Bible as a whole. He will not tell you to do something that will bring spiritual harm to another person or that will function as a stumbling block to others. John wrote: "He who loves his brother abides in the light, and there is no cause for stumbling in him" (1 John 2:10).

When God reveals His specific answer to your specific question, you then have a responsibility to act upon that answer.

• *Recall a time in your life when you turned to the Scriptures for a specific answer to a question or problem you had and you received an answer from God's Word.*

_____

_____

What the Word Says

[Jesus said]: "To whom much is given, from him much will be required." (Luke 12:48)

Be doers of the word, and not hearers only, deceiving yourselves. For if anyone is a hearer of the word and not a doer, he is like a man observing his natural face in a mirror; for he observes himself, goes away, and immediately forgets what kind of man he was. But he who looks into the perfect law of liberty and continues in it, and is not a forgetful hearer but a doer of the work, this one will be blessed in what he does. (James 1:22–25)

[Jesus said]: "Therefore whoever hears these sayings of Mine, and does them, I will liken him to a wise man who built his house on the rock; and the rain descended, the floods came, and the winds blew and beat on that house; and it did not fall, for it was founded on the rock. But everyone who hears these sayings of Mine, and does not do them, will be like a foolish man who built his house on the sand; and the rain descended, the floods came, and the winds blew and beat on that house; and it fell. And great was its fall." (Matt. 7:24–27)

Teach me Your way, O LORD; I will walk in Your truth. (Ps. 86:11)

What the Word Says to Me

Answers Are Encouraging!

When God answers our questions about our identity, and when He provides direction for us to take in puzzling situations, we cannot help but feel encouraged! We have been given a purpose in life. We have a job that we are equipped to do and can succeed at doing as we trust the Holy Spirit. Our lives can be filled with meaning, and we can know the satisfaction that comes with serving God effectively.

One of the foremost ways you can encourage others is to tell them these two truths:

- God has a purpose for your life. He has gifted you in special ways to do a specific job.
- God has an answer to your questions. He wants you to live in His wisdom, day by day, situation by situation.

You may not have answers to the questions that people ask you, including your children, but you can always say, "I don't know. But I know the One who does! Let's ask God." Be quick to pray with others that they might turn to God for the answers they need to the big questions about their lives, and to the immediate questions they have about their circumstances. Be quick to point others toward the riches of God's Word—it is the Answer Book to life's most puzzling test questions.

- *In what ways are you being challenged today to encourage others? Is there someone specific to whom God is calling you to share the answers that are found in having a relationship with Him? Is God calling you to point someone toward the Word of God for answers to their questions?*

_____

_____

CONCLUSION

PEACE AND JOY ARE GOD'S PLAN!

The word *encourage* means literally "to put courage into another person." We share encouragement with others so that they might have more courage to live *victoriously* in this world. In turn, we are encouraged as we read God's Word, the supreme message of encouragement.

Reconsider the themes in this study book:

- You are loved by God.
- You can receive forgiveness.
- You are destined for eternal life in heaven.
- God is in absolute control and we can trust Him to make a way where there is no way.
- God enables you by the power of the Holy Spirit to live a victorious life over evil and to lead a virtuous life.
- You can live in freedom from evil, and live in freedom to pursue your God-given potential and to serve others.
- You are being changed into the likeness of Jesus Christ.
- God will make a way through any storm you experience.
- God will give you His answer, His wisdom, His counsel.

What wonderful promises we have been given in God's Word. God Himself is our Supreme Encourager! He is the One who imparts courage to us so that we might face life with an assurance that all things *are* being worked together for our highest and eternal good (Rom. 8:28).

When we allow ourselves truly to be encouraged by God's Word, two things happen in us:

1. We experience an abiding sense of God's peace and joy at the very deepest level of our being.
2. We have a growing desire to share God's Word with others.

If you are *not* experiencing God's peace and joy today, ask God to show you why you aren't. His desire is that you rest fully in Him and that you have an exhilaration about your life and a hope for your future. He wants you to have courage that flows from knowing fully that He is present with You and will never leave you nor forsake you.

Allow yourself to be encouraged. Choose to take in God's promises and receive God's encouragement.

And then, what you have received from God, freely share with others. Every person you meet—today and every day—needs the encouragement that you are equipped to give.